The Green Lamp

Mishka Zakharin

TrIndie Publishing
www.trindiepublishing.com

LCCN: 2011941821
ISBN: 978-0-9835204-4-3

Printed on acid-free paper in the United States of America

"He was one of those idealistic Russians who, struck by some compelling idea, immediately become entirely obsessed by it for ever. They are quite incapable of mastering it, but believe in it passionately, and so their whole life passes afterwards, as it were, in the last agonies under the weight of a heavy stone which has fallen upon them and half crushed them."

—Fyodor Dostoyevsky
from 'The Devils'
[translated by David Magarshack]

Table of Contents

Table of Contents

Dostoyevsky for Children: Crime & Punishment
. . . inspired by the writings of Feodor Dostoyevsky

Chapter One

Is it wrong to put someone in a box? Rodion Romanovitch Raskolnikov wondered to himself. *No matter how much that person might deserve it? What if there are mice and rats in the box! How horrible . . . to lure one into a box, perhaps drop her shoes inside and then offer to hold it open while she retrieves them then—BAM!—slam shut the lid! Trapped! While she's gnawed upon by hungry rodents . . .*

But what about Napoleon? A tyrant who nearly conquered all of Europe—shouldn't someone have put him in a box? I should rather think so, rats or no! I mean, if you know doing something—such as putting someone in a box—is wrong, doesn't it make it all right if the one who is being boxed is somehow . . . wronger?

As he approached, slowly climbing the stairway to the fourth floor, Raskolnikov began to feel the twitcherings of nervousness...*but why all the fuss*, he thought, waving it all away with a laugh. He was out to pawn his watch, after all, nothing more.

He hesitated only a moment, taking a deep breath before knocking at the pawnbroker woman's door. It flew open instantly as if she had been waiting just inside, and knew, just somehow mystically *knew*, someone was there—and Raskolnikov took an involuntary half-step backward. *The witch!* He forced himself to smile at the old woman's scowling visage.

"Alyona Ivanovna!" he greeted her, offering half a bow. "I have come to pawn my watch."

With a grunt, Alyona Ivanovna stepped aside to allow Raskolnikov to enter. He had been there before—when he had pawned various other items in the preceding months—but he looked about her apartment now with a keener eye.

"What a beautiful day, eh?" said Raskolnikov, strolling casually over to the window and seeming to gaze out as his peripheral vision took note of all that lay within the confines of the dismal apartment. The main area was a fairly good-sized room with three other rooms coming off of it. He tried to decide where she would keep her treasures—where the loot would be hidden—not in the main room, surely. Turning back to her, he took note of a large key hanging on a chain about her neck. *Ah, ha!* He was beginning to sweat. "I took the scenic route coming here, along toward Petrovsky Island"

He was cut off by the old woman. "Bah! Just show me the watch," she said, holding out her hand and shaking it at him impatiently.

"Of course," Raskolnikov agreed quickly. He took it out—a fine, antique, pocket watch and chain—and laid it in her hand.

"It is an inheritance from my father," he explained. "I hate to let it go—but a fellow has to eat, eh?" He forced a laugh, but it came off sounding all French and phony, so he stopped. "So . . . how much do you suppose I can get for it?"

Alyona Ivanovna grunted indignantly. Hoisting up the hem of her dress, a rippling flatulence was emitted from beneath and she spat on Raskolnikov. "A ruble and a half."

"A ruble and a half?" Raskolnikov repeated, wiping the spit from his face with the sleeve of his coat. "Oh, surely you can offer more than that! It . . . it was my father's—"

"A ruble and a half—take it or leave it!"

Raskolnikov sighed. "Very well, I suppose I really have no choice." Suppressing a smile, he added, "I am at your mercy."

The woman barked out a harsh, humorless laugh. "I have none of that, young man!"

She waddled off into the next room with his watch. Raskolnikov pretended not to pay attention to what she was about, but he took careful note of her every move. She took a small chest out from under the bed and opened it with the key she wore around her neck. Inside he could see—even from the next room—a number of other shiny, sparkling items within. She put Raskolnikov's watch inside, then closed and locked the chest. Taking yet another key out of her apron pocket, she used it to unlock the top drawer to the bureau beside the bed and took out several coins. Returning to the main room, she thrust them at Raskolnikov.

"There—a ruble and a half! I'll probably lose money at such a price for a watch like that . . . now get out and don't come back unless you have something of value to sell me!"

The old witch continued to squawk at him, waving and pushing and kicking him toward the door, and the moment he was outside, she slammed the door shut before he could utter another word.

As he descended the stairs from Alyona Ivanovna's apartment, Raskolnikov gripped the coins tightly in his fist. *Surely*, he thought, *the world would be better if a vile, old harpy like that were put away in a box somewhere . . .*

Chapter Two

Raskolnikov had much to consider. He had had to drop out of the university due to a lack of funds and he had been feeling increasingly ill of late, such that he was unable, or unwilling, to find work. But now inspiration—albeit misguided—had offered a solution. He could lock the old pawnbroker woman Alyona Ivanovna away in a box, and, in having done the world (or, at the very least, St. Petersburg) such a favor, he would abscond with her treasures. He justified his plot by telling himself she had practically stolen it all anyway from the poor and needy who are forced to part with their jewelry and heirlooms and whatnot, simply to buy food or clothes and merely go on existing.

"Napoleon . . ." he mused, as he wandered along the streets aimlessly. "Ah, Napoleon—you would have done it, wouldn't you? You'd have put the old hag into a box and shut her up in it forever! Because you were a great man, out to accomplish great deeds, and what matter if a few eggs get broken when you're out to make an omelet, eh? (Not that you, in your own right, didn't deserve a box of your own, however!)"

Not wishing to return home yet—for what, he thought, did he have to return to anyway? He ducked into a tavern for a glass of vodka and a taco and was immediately accosted.

"May I join you?" a man asked—though not really asking so much as just doing so, as he sat down directly beside Raskolnikov. "I'd love a bit of conversation! Uh! Isn't it grand—words, words, words, words! And you seem the scholarly type—you're a student, aren't you? Ha! I knew it!" The man grabbed his glass of vodka and raised it in salute. "To the *intelligent-sia*!" He downed it all in a gulp and immediately poured another glass, also topping off Raskolnikov's, though the latter indicated it was not necessary. "Indeed, the only thing I really enjoy more than a good conversation is a bit of *potatoey libation*, eh?" The man grinned mischievously, jiggling his glass and leaning right in down low by Raskolnikov's lap. Raskolnikov inched away a bit. "But where are my manners! I am Marmeladov, my good man . . . and you are . . .?"

"Oh . . . um, Raskolnikov."

"Uh! An exemplary name! Oh, I'm such a clod of dirt . . ."

Raskolnikov blinked away his surprise as the exuberant man before him, who quite suddenly deflated away into nothing (though not literally, of course). "Well, whatever is the matter?" he asked.

"I am nothing, nothing, I tell you! Once . . . well, maybe once I could have been something. I worked as a government clerk, you know, or I suppose, you wouldn't, as we've just met, my dear friend! My wife, the lovely and consumptive Katerina Ivanovna, married beneath her station when she signed on with me, I can tell you, but we loved one another and I tried to make her happy . . ." Marmeladov gulped down another glass of vodka, again immediately refilling. "But I spun away everything we had . . ."

"Spun it away?"

"Oh, yes!" The man's eyes blazed. "You see, you stand out in an open area, stretch your arms wide, and then spin and spin and spin and spin until you can't stand or walk or anything, and then you fall down and (sometimes) vomit."

"Oh, my! That does sound exciting!"

"Positively intoxicating . . . that's what *this* is for," he said, indicating the vodka. "It's the only thing to keep me from getting dizzy."

"It must be horrible," said Raskolnikov, and truly meant it.

"Yes, wasted away every last kopek—including the money my dear and consumptive Katerina Ivanovna brought with her from her first marriage, mind you. Almost all was spent on doctor's bills from when I would fall and hit my head—or to buy new shirts when I'd vomited all down the front of myself. Oh! I am but the maggots and stench about a dead dog rotting in the street!"

Marmeladov dropped his head onto his hands upon the table and began to sob. After several very uncomfortable minutes in which Raskolnikov did not at all know how to react, Marmeladov abruptly sat up straight, drank yet another glass of vodka (and yet again refilled his glass) and stared directly into Raskolnikov's eyes.

"But enough about me. Tell me about yourself, my new friend." He put on a smile, waiting patiently for Raskolnikov to begin.

"Oh, well, let's see . . ." said Raskolnikov, uneasily. "I've been in Petersburg now for—"

"And then!" Marmeladov declared, rising in his seat, "and *then* . . . with three small children at home to feed, I lose my government job. And just two years before I can claim my pension, mind you—and my beloved and consumptive Katerina Ivanovna forces my darling daughter (from my first marriage, now), my darling daughter Sonia Semyonovna, to take up the *yellow feather*!"

Raskolnikov shuddered, unable to refrain from grasping the arm of the poor, distraught, ruined man beside him. *Marmeladov's daughter forced into prostitution!? Tickling men's (or women's, presumably) asses with a big, yellow feather . . . for money! What happens with feathers between a man and his wife is one thing—or even between just any two consenting adults, really—or, perhaps, two women, a young boy and a goat*, he thought, remembering the trials of his own adolescence . . . *but to do so for money—in the absence of love!?*

"You poor, dear soul . . ." muttered Raskolnikov, pouring more vodka into the man. "Let me get you home."

Chapter Three

Upon returning to his own home, Raskolnikov was confronted by Nastasya, the cook at his apartment building. It seemed Praskovya Pavlovna had been complaining that Raskolnikov was still behind in his rent, and she was very soon going to go the police about it. Further, she told Nastasya to stop bringing Raskolnikov food.

"She'll never evict me," Raskolnikov told Nastasya. "We're practically family, she and I." He was referring to his previous engagement to Praskovya Pavlovna's daughter, who had only the last year become very ill and been put in a box. The betrothal, of course, given the circumstances, had been called off.

"Well, that's between you and her, I suppose," said Nastasya. "I'll not get involved with it—nor will I let a man starve. You probably haven't eaten in days, have you?"

"I just had a taco a little while ago . . ."

"Taco! I'll go get you some real food—cabbage soup and maybe some nice turnip and vodka pie, hmmm?" She turned to leave, but quite suddenly spun back around. "Hup! Almost forgot—you received a letter." She took the letter out of her apron pocket and handed it to him, taking leave and closing the door behind her.

Raskolnikov tore open the envelope—it was a letter from his mother and thirty rubles. He immediately felt a pang of guilt; it had been months since he'd written to her and his sister Dounia, but then he remembered he'd been very busy lying about and thinking of things . . .

My Dear Rodya,

There is so much to tell you, I hardly know where to begin. I must warn you, some of my news seems very bad on the surface, but in the end all has turned out really very well.

Your sister Dounia has been dismissed from her position as governess to Marfa Petrovna's children. Marfa Petrovna's husband, Mr. Svidrigailov, had gotten the notion into his head that he would like to tickle your sister's ass with a feather—and, of course (in all likelihood), to have her tickle his ass with a feather as well. When poor Dounia tried to tell Marfa Petrovna about it, Mr. Svidrigailov managed to twist everything around and make it sound as if the whole ass-tickling idea had been Dounia's in the first place! And so she was dismissed and sent home in disgrace. Marfa Petrovna then slandered Dounia's reputation all about town, and . . . well, perhaps I shouldn't say . . . but . . . well . . . your dear sister took to spinning for a time—though she's stopped now, so I suppose that's all right then.

Fortunately, one of Marfa Petrovna's servants found a letter that her husband had written to Dounia and the dreadful Mr. Svidrigailov was found out. Marfa Petrovna felt extremely remorseful and made amends to Dounia by going herself from house to house all about town to clear her reputation. Marfa Petrovna has also arranged for Dounia to marry her cousin Pyotr Petrovich Luzhin. It is the hope of both your sister and myself that Mr. Luzhin, who is a man of some means, will perhaps help to pay for your university tuition, and perhaps to even aid you in finding employment!

So, you see, even through such adversity everything has certainly turned out for the best! We will be arriving in St. Petersburg to visit very soon, at which time you shall meet Mr. Luzhin, who is already there on business. We are very happy and excited that we will be seeing you after so long! You are always in our prayers, both Dounia's and my own. You mean more to us than we do even to each other (but, of course, you know how your sister can be . . .). Enclosed, as well, are thirty rubles; I had hoped to send more, but we will need the extra for traveling to Petersburg.

Yours 'til death,
Pulcheria Raskolnikov (i.e. 'Mom')

By the time he had finished the letter, Raskolnikov was shaking.

"So that's what they think of me!" he fumed, through gritted teeth. "I can see straight through her intricate machinations—they hate me! They *loathe* me!"

Crumpling up the ruble-notes and casting them to the floor, he immediately picked them back up again (because, after all, money is money) and shoved it all deep into his pockets. Fearing apoplexy, he ran from his room and out into the streets. He made his way along Vassilyevsky Prospect, persuading his anger to conform to rationality.

"No, no, of course they don't hate me. I'm a fool!"

He stopped to kick himself in the leg.

Mother is oblivious, that much is clear, but Dounia? Dounia throws her life away for me! She's no different than Sonia Semyonovna, that poor, yellow-feathered daughter of Marmeladov! Only she's worse—for Sonia Semyonovna tickles asses to survive, to buy food and clothing and shelter for herself and her family, but Dounia—oh, Dounia! That silly little whore! She throws her life away to tickle some old bore's ass to bargain for luxuries!

At that moment a whirling blue object flew past him, nearly knocking him to the ground. Catching hold of himself, Raskolnikov realized it was a young woman (in a blue dress), spinning wildly out of control as she ran along the street. Pulled from his private thoughts, he now noticed how everyone all around was staring at the spectacle, pointing and laughing or shaking their heads sadly. And his own foolish sister had been spinning as well, he remembered, though supposedly had quit. He thought of Marmeladov, the poor man, how he had given his life over to the spinning, and the only thing to keep him sane and sober anymore was the vodka.

Raskolnikov wondered if Napoleon had ever spun about so.

Upon thinking of the infernal dictator, Raskolnikov was confounded by the naughtiest of desires. Stealing away to a secluded pathway in the park, he glanced around to see if anyone was about. Seeing it was clear, he spread wide his arms and twirled madly about! Twirling and swirling and spinning and grinning and sure (really quite positive) that he absolutely must vomit at any moment! But then suddenly he lost his footing and fell, hitting his head on a bench or something, and rolling into the bushes, unconscious.

Raskolnikov was a child again—tied to a tree in his native province of R___ . . . there was a black duck, black as pitch, black as darkest night with no moon or stars and your eyes closed as well, and the duck was cursing at Raskolnikov in French while a feral badger, with fiery red eyes and foam bubbling from its stinking maw, poked at him with a stick . . . and then a great, angry boar in a fez—symbolic, no doubt, he realized later, of the repression of the common man by the engorged and unrelentingly dastardly, bastardly overlords in authority—arrived with a giant box, saying they were going to put Raskolnikov into it and leave him only rats (or perhaps a vole or two) as company . . .

Raskolnikov woke with a start, only to discover squirrels nibbling at his extremities. Brushing them away, he scurried from out the bushes.

"Well, I'm resolved then," he decided aloud. "I shall go forth with my experiment, but I'll be very certain there are no rats or voles . . ." He shuddered and brushed his sleeve as though it might fling the terrible dream off of him. ". . . or squirrels! No *ookey* rodents of any sort in the box with her!"

Chapter Four

Raskolnikov felt himself really rather fortunate to have managed to tote such a big box along through the streets of St. Petersburg without drawing unwanted attention. Nastasya had *almost* glimpsed him as he left the apartment building, but had then been distracted away by a kitten trying to escape from the soup she was preparing. He was concerned as he dragged the large box up the stairs of Alyona Ivanovna's building, fearful of all the noise it was making, scraping along behind him, but destiny was on his side, he could feel it. Even the painters who had been working in the empty flat beneath the insidious pawnbroker's rooms were conveniently away.

Boldly knocking at the door, he waited, growing quickly impatient and knocking again and again, wondering why she wasn't answering. She had nearly pounced out at him the last time. What was taking her so long now?! Beginning to whimper, he was about to bolt away—to abandon the box and his plans and just flee—when the door creaked open merely a crack, enough for Alyona Ivanovna's beady little eyes to glare out at him.

"Who are you?" she growled. "What do you want?"

"It is I, Raskolnikov," he said grandly, his eyes wide with frenzy, but not a quaver in his voice. "I have something to pawn," he continued, pushing open the door, forcing her out of the way and striding into the room, his box in tow.

"What is it then?" she demanded, staring at the large box. "More worthless trinkets?!"

"Oh, no, no, no!" Raskolnikov laughed. "It isn't in the box! That's just . . ." His mind went blank. ". . . I'm going to buy some jam!" he decided, suddenly. "And this is for carrying it home . . . after I've gotten the money, I mean . . . after I've pawned my...silver cigarette case!" He fumbled to pull a small cigarette case shaped package from his pocket (which was really not at all a cigarette case, but merely a prop in his masterful subterfuge to throw the devious old woman off his scent!). "It was my auntie's, you see, but . . . well, she smoked like a fish, she did! *Ha-ha!* And so now she's dead."

"She's *what?!*" the old woman flinched with surprise.

"No! I mean—that is—" Raskolnikov stole a guilty glance down at the box. "She's gone to America and—"

"Bah!" Alyona Ivanovna waved off his explanation and snatched the package from his hands. "Fish don't smoke . . ." she muttered.

"Oh! No, no, of course not," Raskolnikov agreed quickly, hoping he hadn't given the game away with his foolish banter. "I simply meant—um— she smoked a lot, is all . . . perhaps I was thinking of smoked fish! *Ha-ha!* Might be good with all that jam I'm going to buy! *Ha-ha-ha!*"

"Well, you've wrapped this tight enough," the old woman groaned, tearing futilely away at the package.

"I think there may be a knife in the box . . ." Raskolnikov suggested, turning toward the large box. "I'll get it for you—oh!—oh!!—I'm suddenly very dizzy . . ."

"Irresponsible youth!" the harpy screeched, thrusting the package back into Raskolnikov's hands as she hiked up her skirt and hoisted herself into the box. "Probably spinning all the way here . . ." she grumbled.

"Oh, wait half a moment," Raskolnikov cautioned her. "Here, here—don't get that key hanging around your neck all tangled up . . . don't want anyone getting hurt . . ." He reveled in how truly concerned for her welfare he sounded.

The woman growled in protest, but slipped the key off the chain and threw it at Raskolnikov. He crammed her down into the box, slammed shut the lid and caught the latch.

It was done.

He breathed a sigh of relief, looking down at his handiwork. He found it amazing that one moment a person could be vile and reprehensible and a hindrance to good people in the world and the next, nothing but an unobtrusive cube that bothers no one.

But there was more yet to do. He took the oversized key and went into the bedroom to raid the woman's treasure chest. He felt rushed to escape for safety before his crime was discovered, and merely grabbed a handful of booty, cramming it into his pockets, *just as he had crammed the old woman into the box!!* He fought off the sudden feeling of revulsion for what he had done . . . after all, he reminded himself, it was all for a higher purpose. He turned his attention to the bureau drawer and suddenly realized he didn't have the key for that!

The old woman must still have it with her in the box!

Too late to do anything about that now . . .

The creak of the front door opening—*as if the shriek of damnation*—froze Raskolnikov in his tracks. For several moments he stood there in the bedroom, feeling his heart pound in his chest, hearing the blood surge in his ears. Then he darted out into the next room to find Alyona Ivanovna's sister Lizaveta staring, pale and wide-eyed, down at the box. She looked up at him and Raskolnikov's resolve faltered. Putting the heinous old woman in a box was one thing, but Lizaveta . . . just a poor, simple, good woman, as much (surely more!) a victim of her sister's evil as anyone else, was an entirely different matter...

But there could be no witnesses to his crime, and he had no time for cleverness. Standing over the box, he loosened the latch, ready to open it. "Get in the box . . ." His voice was stern, but his eyes pleaded with her. He knew it would have to be fast—she would practically have to dive in, with Raskolnikov slamming the lid shut on her heels, or Alyona Ivanovna could escape. "It's the only way . . ." he assured her.

"The only way . . ." she agreed.

When the deed was done, he managed to sneak out of the building undetected. He made his way home, taking a very sporadic and random route, and then he spun around until he truly did vomit. When he awoke, it was three days later and his room was filled with people . . .

Chapter Five

Of course, it did not take all that many people to fill Raskolnikov's room. Being only eight feet wide by ten feet long, it contained a sofa (also used as his bed), a small writing table upon which sat half a dozen books, and three chairs (one of which was broken, and the sitter had to brace himself against the wall or would inevitably fall over). So, although upon first waking he was startled to find his room "filled with people," in truth there were only three others. His first thought was for the jewelry and baubles he'd liberated from the old pawnbroker woman, but his panic was quickly assuaged as he recalled stuffing it all in a hole in the wall where the wallpaper had begun peeling away; he could see the spot from where he lay, just there by the table leg, and it did not seem to have been disturbed.

"He's awake!" announced Nastasya, cutting off the hiss of whispered conversation. "Raskolnikov, we were so worried about you! Here, I've brought you a sausage!"

"Let him breathe, for pity's sake!" The speaker was Razumihin, a friend of Raskolnikov and a fellow student; until recently he had helped Razumihin translate books from French or German or English into Russian, but Raskolnikov hadn't been to see him now for over four months. They had only ever met at the university—he was certainly quite surprised to see him here! "Here, now, here, now! Well! Certainly glad to see you with your eyes open, my friend!" Razumihin said. "You've been out for three days. Another two and we were going around to order you a box!"

Raskolnikov paled at the suggestion, and he was pale enough already, but his even paler complexion now caused Razumihin to gasp and Nastasya to throw her sausage at the spectral man lying before her.

"A . . . a box!?" Raskolnikov said. *Surely they know! Why do they taunt me so! Why don't they just drag me away in chains and be done with it!* Banishing the haranguery of his chaotic musings, he said, "Raz . . . how . . ." He was unsure even where to begin! He tried again. "What are you—"

"What am I doing here? How did I find you?" Razumihin responded, laughing boyishly. "Well, it wasn't difficult. I spied you several weeks ago in the neighborhood, and so I inquired at a few of the local taverns until I found someone who knew you—a man by the name of Marmeladov?"

It took Raskolnikov half a moment to recall the name, his mind still a bit foggy, but he nodded agreement.

"Uh!" Razumihin said, hitting his forehead with the heel of his hand. "But where are my manners!" Waving forward the third visitor, who had been standing silent vigil beside the door, Razumihin said, "Rodion Raskolnikov, I present Ivan Karamazov Ivan, this is Rodya . . ."

"Razumihin has told me much of you," said Ivan with a formal sort of half a bow. "It is a privilege to meet you."

"And for I," Raskolnikov replied automatically.

"Quite a coincidence," broke in Razumihin, seeming (as usual) over-ly amused, finding you through your friend Marmeladov, I mean. You see, Ivan here used to be married to your friend's wife!"

Raskolnikov frowned. "Katerina Ivanovna?!"

"The same," Ivan agreed, nodding his head. "The beautiful and (at the time) non-consumptive."

"But…I thought her first husband had been put into a box!?"

"Certainly, certainly, and such is how I made it appear to her," Ivan explained, a mournful tone in his voice. "I did truly love her when first we were wed—don't believe for a moment I did not! But, after only a year of marriage, I discovered I was incapable of the sort of love she deserved. She was very well-to-do you know and her needs so very magnanimous, so I faked putting myself into a box, but of course leaving her an extremely generous inheritance."

"Which Marmeladov then spun all away, leaving them destitute!" The pieces were beginning to fit together for Raskolnikov. Feathers came to mind and he suddenly felt very twitchy. He shuddered violently and sat up, throwing off the blanket. "That must have been very difficult for you," Raskolnikov sympathized.

Ivan shrugged. "Life at times requires sacrifice," Ivan said. "One must be prepared to suffer personal hardships if it may benefit the greater good."

Raskolnikov blinked back his surprise at Ivan's choice of words. "The greater good, you say?"

"Indeed!" Ivan said, scratching at his beard and pursing his lips in a moment of severe introspection. "You see, although life is filled with beauty—and what could be more beautiful than love, eh?—still, beauty is intuitive, from within, and therefore cannot be trusted entirely."

"Astonishing!" declared Raskolnikov. "But then, if not one's own intuition, what can one trust?"

"Logic!" Ivan said. His eyes blazed and he became really very hard. "It is reason that creates a trustworthy synthesis of inner and outer know-ledge."

"A conjoining of intuitive—including emotive—thought," Raskolnikov added, biting at his lips, working it all through, "with observational knowledge? But what if one is unsure if it is reason or intuition that guides him?"

"Then surely the path is clear, for if it leads from *both* . . ." Ivan shrugged off the foregone conclusion.

"I see, but what if I—" Raskolnikov caught himself, silently willing the others not to have noticed. "That is . . . what if *someone* . . . just some random fellow, mind you, what if he is mad?"

"Ah!" Ivan declared, significantly. "*That* then is quite a pickle! I suppose the *logical* end that should be met, is the madman must play out the role he has found for himself. For what else can any of us do?"

"Yes?" prompted Raskolnikov.

"And it is up to those around him—and I mean of course, those who are by common consensus deemed to be in their right minds—these people should put the poor fellow in a box or something?"

"I say!" burst in Razumihin. "For madness!?"

"Certainly! If not for him, the madman himself, then, indeed, for the cause of the greater good!"

"Indeed," agreed Raskolnikov, feeling really very smarmy at this point. "The greater good . . ." Raskolnikov found himself again thinking of Napoleon . . . *What the dickens did he have in his breast pocket anyway?!*

"Well, I think it's barbaric," offered Razumihin, "to box a man simply because he's out of his gourd?"

"Who was it," continued Ivan, "who wrote: 'We are yet, and shall always be, the primitives we started off as . . . it is only the act of pretending to be appalled by our savage natures that has become more elaborate. We are but actors, feigning sainthood, as we revel in sin . . . enslaved to the burdens of corporeity'?"

Raskolnikov and Razumihin exchanged a glance and shrugged their ignorance. "Yes, well—no, I have no idea," Razumihin admitted.

"Nor do I," replied Ivan, significantly, "nor do I . . ."

"Well, if you ask me," said Nastasya, who had been sitting quietly in the corner fondling Raskolnikov's sausage, "you all make about as much sense as Rodya's ranting when he was delirious with fever!"

"Ranting!?" Raskolnikov gasped. Raskolnikov's earlier chaotic haranguery rose once more to the surface. "What . . . whatever was I ranting about?"

"Oh, just a lot of rubbish," Razumihin reassured him. "Most of it was incoherent. There was something about a box—which was especially odd, as your fingers were filled with slivers." With a sharp burst of laughter, he added, "And then Nastasya—dear Nastasya!—began flying all about shouting 'The Stigmata! The Stigmata! Christ the Carpenter—Lord have mercy!' And I had to have Ivan beat her with a stick to calm her down!"

Raskolnikov glanced at Nastasya who frowned sheepishly.

"I'm better now," she said.

Ivan shrugged.

"But that's neither here nor there," Razumihin declared, waving away the entire conversation to that point. "I expected you and Ivan would hit it off. You're each so very philosophical and moody, and I see now I was correct, which is why I have a proposal. Ivan has been helping me with some translations and I have just recently received copies of several new books from various German authors. I thought I might see if you could help us with their translations—splitting the fee even-up, three ways, of course." A wry grin crept over his face and he added, "Although, I certainly didn't expect to find you here like this—in such a state!"

"And he's been such a help," chimed in Nastasya. "Mr. Razumihin has rarely left your bedside while we've been nursing you back to health, and he even brought you new clothes!"

"Oh, pish-posh—fiddlety-doo!" said Razumihin, waving away her praises. "The least I could do. You'd do the same for me I'm sure, and anyway, they're hardly *new* clothes—new to you perhaps, but still better than the vomit-encrusted ones you had on when we found you! But now that you're awake, I must be off. There are others who await the news of your 'resurrection'."

"Your mother and sister are here," said Nastasya at the unasked question of Raskolnikov's furrowed brow. "Well, not *here* here, but at the boarding house on the next block; they arrived just yesterday, and oh what a state your mother was in to find you like this!"

"Well, I'd best not linger then," said Razumihin, grabbing his hat and heading out the door. "Think about my proposal! I'll be back soon!"

"Yes, yes, that would be best," said Raskolnikov, his head swimming with thoughts, his spleen rising uncomfortably. "I. . .I'm feeling so much better, but I think . . . I think I'd like to rest a bit yet."

"Of course, of course," replied Nastasya. "We'll leave you alone now." She wiped the sausage off on her skirt and set it on the table. "I'll just leave this here for you for after your rest."

Following the others out, Ivan Karamazov stopped in the doorway and turned to glance back at Raskolnikov. "I see you, Rodya Raskolnikov." And, with a wink, he too was gone.

Chapter Six

"They know! They all know, they must!" Raskolnikov groaned to himself when the others had gone. He jumped from the sofa and began pacing nervously back and forth across his room. "Such a cruel game they play, and all to make my senses crack! They toy with me—because they're jealous! They know what I have done, what it means! 'Greater good', indeed! (And what was that 'I see you' crap all about!?) They at last see me for who and what I am, a man of reckoning! A man of destiny!!"

His eyes were drawn to the hole where he had stashed his treasure trove. He hurriedly dug it all out and put it in his coat pocket.

"When they've had their fun, taunting me with their feigned ignorance over my actions, they'll come searching for evidence, hard evidence. They'll burst in and heave me to the floor, bludgeon me, spit on me and ransack the place until they find what they're looking for! (For all the good it will do them!!) But they'll not find anything here! I'll take it and bury it someplace—under a rock somewhere where no one will ever suspect!"

Sneaking out of his room, he made sure Nastasya was not about and quickly made it out the front door of the apartment building without being detected.

Now, he thought, *to find the perfect hiding place. Oh, they may think they're clever, finding me out—however it was they did—but I'll yet get away with it. They may think they have me, but they'd best think again! They may know all about it now, but I'll not let them know that I know they know. Ha! And then soon, perhaps, they shall all forget . . . and maybe I shall have never known!*

After finding an appropriate hiding place for his plunder—and making sure to note the exact location so he could retrieve it later—Raskolnikov wandered about the city in a haze of delirium. The world seemed to swirl all around him as if he'd had a vigorous spin and was just on the verge of either vomiting or losing consciousness.

Perhaps a touch of vodka, he decided, *just to clear my thoughts, just to help regain my focus . . .*

As he approached the tavern across from his apartment building, however, Raskolnikov found himself in the midst of a commotion in the street. In his confused state, he had blundered into the middle of it inadvertently, but he suddenly realized he was standing on something—or *someone*—and someone he knew!

"Marmeladov!" he exclaimed, stepping from the man's chest and crouching down beside him. "What are you doing down there? I was just going in for some vodka, if you'd care to join me . . . are you all right?"

Marmeladov opened his mouth to speak, but all that was emitted was a slight wheeze as a dark pink spit-bubble slowly grew from his lips. Raskolnikov poked it with his finger and it popped, sending a fine splay of red across the face of Marmeladov, who then passed out with a dull groan.

"He must have been spinning quite a lot, the way he staggered all about like that," Raskolnikov heard spoken by someone in the crowd. He felt somewhat relieved that he had not in some way been responsible for his friend's misfortune—and yet he knew the stranger's observation to be correct; he could see the wear of centrifugal velocity all over Marmeladov's clothes.

"Oh, dear," Raskolnikov muttered. "We must get him home—quickly! Someone please help, he lives very near."

By the time they got the broken Marmeladov home, Raskolnikov's head was clear, his illness seeming to have entirely abated, which was just as well, as the over-wrought and consumptive Katerina Ivanovna was, as might be expected, thoroughly distraught to see her husband in such a state.

"So you are Raskolnikov?" she said, weeping into his shoulder. "Yes, yes, my poor, dear, deluded husband has mentioned you."

She paused to cough up a most horrendous gob of bloody mucous onto Raskolnikov's shirt. He held her closer to prevent himself from shuddering with disgust. It wasn't her fault, he told himself, it was the consumption—the tiny, demonic parasites in her lungs that were consuming her from within. There would be other shirts.

"What happened? Someone, please—what happened to my poor, stupid lout of a husband?"

"I saw the whole thing," said one of the men who had helped to carry Marmeladov. "He came running out of the tavern across the way, spinning and singing and spilling his vodka all about—then suddenly from around the corner, a run-away horse came flying, running him down and both horse and cart went right over the top of him!"

"Oh, the poor, dumb fool!" Katerina sobbed, pounding on her unconscious husband's chest. "He never was good with animals."

"Please, please, make way," shouted a man, making his way through the throng of spectators in the doorway. "Please, I'm a doctor!"

"Doctor Zossimov!" Raskolnikov exclaimed, surprised but pleased to see his own physician. Raskolnikov stepped forward to help pull the man through. "Yes, hurry, do you think he has a chance?"

"Oh, this is horrible! Horrible!" gasped the doctor after quickly inspecting the patient. As he was poking and prodding about, determining the extent of the damage, Marmeladov began to groan, his bleary eyes fluttering weakly half open. "Okay, now, just hold still," the doctor said, "we'll do all we can for you." Standing to address Raskolnikov and Katerina, the doctor continued, saying, "Well, he's awakened, and that's certainly a good sign."

"Then he'll be all right?" asked Katerina. "The poor, unlucky bastard will be okay?"

"No, I'm afraid we'll need a box at any moment. The damage is just too great, and unfortunately it almost looks as though he might have gotten off with just a couple of broken legs, a broken arm, and a concussion, perhaps a shattered jaw—but it's almost as if someone had been standing on his chest! Now he has fractured ribs poking into his lungs, and—oh! It's just horrible!" He shook his head sadly, gazing down at Katerina Ivanovna as she tried as best she could to make her husband comfortable. "I could bleed him, if you'd like," the doctor offered.

"Will it help?" asked Raskolnikov, hopefully.

"It seems unlikely."

"Yes, yes, of course—then bleed him right away!"

"Hup, too late!" the doctor said. "His frazzled and consumptive wife has already got him in the box. Well, anyway, I don't suppose it would have mattered."

"Oh! Oohhh!" groaned Katerina, softly petting her husband's box. "However shall we go on? We could use it as a coffee table, couldn't we? Not that we can afford the coffee to put on it! I can't believe he's gone." She again interrupted herself with a fit of coughing—hacking up a bloody gob that splattered straight into Raskolnikov's eye. It seemed impossible for him to get his mind around the knowledge that this shell of a woman, this victim of such extreme poverty, had once been the beautiful, well-to-do bride of his new acquaintance Ivan Karamazov! "Well," she sighed, "at least I suppose now the children will have something to eat."

Raskolnikov, not knowing what else to do, started to leave, but was stopped by a young woman, very pretty in a plain sort of manner and perhaps no more than seventeen or eighteen years old. Her soft, pale lips held a melancholy smile that tugged at Raskolnikov's heart-strings. He knew instinctively that this must be Marmeladov's daughter, the yellow-feathered Sonia Semyonovna.

"You are a very kind man," she said, taking Raskolnikov's hand. As she did so, her feather, protruding slightly from out her sleeve, tickled his wrist—a spasm of giddiness passed through him and he had the mad impulse to grab her into his embrace and spin all about the room with her! The mere thought made him dizzy. He side-stepped slightly, catching his balance and brushing a leg against her father's box. There was a hollow groan from within, which no one else seemed to hear, and Raskolnikov allowed his impulse to pass unindulged. He offered a squeeze of condolence instead, before taking back his hand.

"Father was very fond of you and spoke of you as a true friend. I see that he was not mistaken," the young girl said sadly.

"I am very sorry about...about all that has happened here . . ." Raskolnikov managed. Remembering the thirty rubles his mother had sent, Raskolnikov quickly fumbled the notes out of his pocket and thrust them into Sonya's hands. "Here, please—it isn't much, but use it for a celebration, in honor of your father . . ."

"You are very kind," muttered Sonya, hardly able to speak, tears of gratitude streaming down her pink cheeks. "You'll come, of course? You have to come!"

"Of course, I shall try, of course."

He tried not to think of feathers.

Chapter Seven

Nearly at the point of utter exhaustion, Raskolnikov returned to his apartment, intending to escape the world and see no one, but no sooner had he dropped onto his sofa, pulling the blanket up over his head, than there was a knock at the door. Even as he resolved to ignore it, the door opened uninvited and a man entered. Raskolnikov eyed him suspiciously.

"May I help you?" he asked, sighing.

The man glanced nervously—or perhaps unapprovingly—about, seeming to find Raskolnikov's accommodations somehow inexcusable.

"Do I know you, sir? I am very ill and can only spare a moment, but—"

"I am Pyotr Petrovich Luzhin," said the man, offering a curt nod of his head. "I am betrothed to your sister."

Adrenaline surged through Raskolnikov, making his spleen itch. "Luzhin, eh?" he said, sitting up and setting the blanket aside. "Please, sit . . ."

Luzhin sat in the broken chair, which promptly fell over, leaving the visitor a crumpled heap on the floor at Raskolnikov's feet. Luzhin hastened to his feet, brushing himself off and muttering that he preferred to stand.

"Would you like a sausage?" Raskolnikov offered. The man, it seemed, might one day be family, after all. Raskolnikov was determined to keep a level head.

"Thank you, no. I thought it appropriate to present myself to you, as I am to wed Dounia. I thought you would want to know the man who is to be your brother-in-law."

Raskolnikov nodded, barely able to make his scowl into a complacent though not at all friendly smirk. "How . . . delightful . . ."

"I assure you, my intentions with regard to your sister are entirely noble," began Luzhin, pacing back and forth before Raskolnikov and staring into his hat. "She is a charming, lovely girl. She seems so very . . . clean . . ." He stopped abruptly, squaring off to face Raskolnikov. "But, I'll have you know, I don't believe in charity. As you are Dounia's brother, I shall of course allow for certain opportunities—but nothing is for free."

Raskolnikov silently considered the man before him. He decided he did not at all like him—and not in an abstract, assumed dislike as before he had met him. There was something about Luzhin that seemed distastefully familiar.

"And what of Dounia herself?" Raskolnikov asked, "Is she to earn her keep as well?"

"Now, now, I see you're agitated by my words. Just hear me out. I am a reasonable man, but to allow someone something for nothing—what does it accomplish? Nothing! It hinders both parties, as each only benefits by half of what they might had they undertaken their endeavors alone. Do you see?"

"And Dounia?"

"Well, of course, with family some allowances must be made. Your sister, by her very nature, will earn her keep. You see, by marrying above her station in life, she will ever after express certain . . . gratitudes upon me, her benefactor."

Raskolnikov slowly stood to face Luzhin eye to eye.

"Gratitudes? Such as perhaps those enacted with a feather!?"

Luzhin's composure melted and he giggled like a school-girl. "Oh, naturally! Or perhaps with pudding!"

Raskolnikov suddenly knew why the man seemed familiar, aside from the outburst of feminine laughter; he was the same sort as the pawnbroker woman Alyona Ivanovna—self-serving, greedy, cold-hearted . . .

"Get out," Raskolnikov growled.

Luzhin frowned.

"I'm afraid I don't understand."

"It's very simple—get out right now!"

Raskolnikov started forward, pushing Luzhin back with the very intensity of his voice.

"Out of my apartment and out of my sister's life!" Standing in the doorway, Luzhin just outside, Raskolnikov added, "And if you still can't understand, I'll show you with the end of my boot, down the stairs!"

Luzhin's eyes grew wide and his mouth gaped. He was clearly unaccustomed to being spoken to in this manner. Without another word, he jammed his hat on top of his head and quickly descended the stairs.

Slamming the door, Raskolnikov paced about the room in a fury, desperately needing an outlet for his rage. He grabbed his sausage and began beating it against his forehead, emitting an anguished groan all the while. So absorbed was he in his exercise, he failed to notice at first that his door had again opened, and (again) a man he did not know entered. As Raskolnikov's frenzy claimed a casualty—the top half of the sausage tearing away and flying across the room—he looked up to see the stranger catch the errant bit of sausage.

"Well done!" said the man, handing back the meaty projectile. "Nothing like a good, hearty sausage pounding for whatever ails you, eh?"

"Who are you?" demanded Raskolnikov, his ire translating instantly into chagrin.

"Forgive the intrusion, of course," said the man, offering a bow. "I am Svidrigailov. Your sister, Dounia, at one time worked as a governess for my children."

Raskolnikov felt as if he might bite through his teeth.

"I'm going to need another sausage!" Raskolnikov snarled.

"Oh, to be sure, to be sure," said Svidrigailov, trying his best to placate Raskolnikov. "But let us not get off on the wrong foot. I have no further interest in Dounia. I came merely to deliver this . . ."

Taking the envelope proffered, Raskolnikov found it full of money.

"And, before you get any ideas about it," Svidrigailov explained, "it is from my wife Marfa Petronova. She had to be put in a box last month. She adored your sister, and the three thousand rubles were hers."

"And even now that your wife is out of the way, you have no further designs over Dounia?" asked Raskolnikov, skeptically. "You could have just sent the money—why travel all the way to Petersburg to deliver it?"

"Well, actually," said Svidrigailov, conspiratorially, his face suddenly aglow. "I have come—to get married! Oh, no, no, I see your concern, but I don't intend your sister . . ."

"Then who?"

"Oh! I don't know yet, perhaps I won't. I haven't really decided yet, perhaps I'll leave Russia entirely. I'm very ill, you see. Perhaps the healing waters at L___ will help…or to winter in Italy . . ."

"Yes, well, I don't see—"

"A puppy!" Svidrigailov interrupted. "Or, no, no—perhaps now I'm just sleepy. I'll go back to my room for a nap."

He moved to leave, but stopped as he reached for the doorknob. "Oh, and this is for your dear sister from me—for the hardships I have caused her . . ."

Raskolnikov took this envelope as well, discovering it to be an even greater amount of money.

"Absolutely not!" He thrust the money back into Svidrigailov's unwanting hands. "I believe I speak for Dounia when I say she wants nothing from you!"

"But ten thousand rubles . . . shouldn't you at least let her make the choice?"

"I'll tell her, but I know already what her answer will be," insisted Raskolnikov, swinging the door open.

After Svidrigailov left, Nastasya informed Raskolnikov that he had been beckoned by the police. Family and money and his sister's suitors forgotten, a dark dread instilled itself within Raskolnikov.

"I must make my escape!" he decided. "The time has come, but to where? America! And *now*, before it all goes to shit . . . but no . . . to flee is as much as an admission of wrong-doing and I have committed no crime, not really. I have done a good deed! Ah, what to do!? I must decide . . . I'll spin first! Yes, I'll spin."

Truly hurling himself into it, in no time at all he was but a whirling dervish of splaying vomit, until suddenly he slipped on a stray piece of sausage and fell head-first into the door.

Chapter Eight

"Now, the reason I've called you here," said the police constable Porfiry Petrovich, "is a very important matter." From where he sat perched on the edge of his desk, he gazed sternly down at Raskolnikov, who waited in sweaty silence for the man to continue. "And it is good that you brought your friend," he continued, indicating Razumihin, whom Raskolnikov had run into on his way to the police station. "It is always good to have a . . . a witness you see . . . for these sorts of . . . delicate matters."

"Yes, yes, of course," Raskolnikov agreed, his throat tight, his mouth feeling as if filled with dirt. "And, if I may ask, what exactly are these . . . delicate matters?"

Porfiry Petrovich went around behind his desk and sat down. Taking up what appeared to be some sort of official-looking document, he silently read it over then waved it before Raskolnikov, explaining, "This is the complaint, you see, that has been lodged against you."

Raskolnikov nodded abruptly, waiting for the boot to drop!

"Oh, really!" said Razumihin, rolling his eyes in exasperation. "Is all this . . . this *drama* really necessary?"

Porfiry Petrovich considered him for half a moment, and abruptly began to laugh. "Oh, surely not! *He-hee!* But what's the fun of police work without a bit of drama, eh? All right then, Mr. Raskolnikov, I'll get to the point."

"Yes, please," said Raskolnikov. *This is it,* he thought, *this is the end!*

"A one Praskovya Pavlovna has issued the complaint that you are indebted to her for over one hundred rubles," declared Porfiry Petrovich, "for back rent on a room you let from her."

"Outstanding debts?!" Raskolnikov exclaimed, thoroughly befuddled. He blinked back his surprise, staring back and forth between Porfiry Petrovich and Razumihin. "That is the reason for this summons!?"

"Well, of course!" replied Porfiry Petrovich, holding back the hint of a chuckle. "And, of course, a lesser charge . . . this same Praskovya Pavlovna has also stated that she has had a sausage go missing . . . she suspects you."

"Oh, well . . . I . . . that is . . ." Raskolnikov again felt flustered, though the warm flush of relief that passed through him allowed him to breathe again, his dread since entering Petrovich's office abated. "I was given the sausage by Nastasya, who works for Praskovya Pavlovna. It wasn't stolen at all!"

"Yes, yes, of course," agreed Porfiry Petrovich. "*He-hee-hee!* We don't, here at the police station, make a habit of persecuting people for being slipped a sausage now and again! *He-hee!* None of our business, you know?"

"Well, I'm sure he's good for it," chimed in Razumihin. "He may not have the money now, but he can certainly get it. Just the other day I offered him work. He's not the type to take advantage of a situation, but he's been very ill, you see."

"Oh, yes, clearly," agreed Porfiry Petrovich. "Just look how red and sweaty he is. But we'll hurry this along so you can get back to convalescing. All I need for you to do is sign this promissory note stating that you intend to fully pay off your debt."

"Oh, yes, right away," said Raskolnikov, taking the paper and signing his name. "As soon as I am completely well again . . ."

"Yes, yes, of course . . . *he-hee!* All seems in order here, then."

Porfiry Petrovich stood to show them to the door, but a thought seemed to occur to him and he hesitated. "But I wonder—if not for your outstanding debt, for what did you think you had been summoned?"

"What did you just do?!" demanded Raskolnikov, panic seizing his heart. Did he have something behind his back? Raskolnikov couldn't tell.

"What! What, me?" asked the startled Porfiry Petrovich.

"You were saying . . . and then . . ."

"Yes? Yes?!"

"No, but I thought you did something, just then . . ."

"Not I!" insisted Porfiry Petrovich. "I've done nothing!"

"But I'm nearly sure of it!"

"Nothing at all—I've just been standing here talking to you."

"He's been very ill," Razumihin reiterated.

"Oh, yes, yes, of course," agreed Porfiry Petrovich. "Very well—*he-hee!*—have a good day."

"Well, then," said Raskolnikov, confused. "I thought you had . . ."

"Yet I protest—for I haven't," replied Porfiry Petrovich. "I have done nothing!"

"What's that behind your back!?" demanded Raskolnikov, leaping forward.

"*ENNGH!!*" cried the constable, jumping away, back behind his desk. "You've frightened me! Now, then, what was your question?"

"What's that behind your back?"

"Well, my front, of course . . . *he-hee!*" Porfiry Petrovich seemed very clever by his answer.

"You make no sense at all!"

"What do you mean?!" asked Porfiry Petrovich, his humor vanishing.

"What do I mean? I have no idea!"

"Ah, well, think on it as a double-negative."

"Ah-ha!" Raskolnikov's stress immediately drained all away. "Well, you're quite right, then, I suppose. I'd never thought of it that way before—to inquire as to what lay *behind* you, I should have said 'in front of your back,' as it is from the contrary direction of your front toward which your back is aimed!"

"*He-hee-hee!*" agreed Porfiry Petrovich, stepping forward to shake Raskolnikov's hand. "Smartly done, my friend!"

"May we go now?" asked Razumihin, who had been waiting impatiently by the door throughout the exchange.

"Yes, yes, of course," said Porfiry Petrovich. "I apologize for keeping you so. Uh! But I've nearly forgotten, you never answered my question. Why is it you thought you had been sent for, if not for your debt?"

"Oh . . . well, I had no idea," replied Raskolnikov. "I certainly didn't think it was because you'd thought I might have put someone in a box—or taken a fist full of valuables from any heinous old woman or anything!"

"Oh, well," said Porfiry Petrovich, "that's a relief! *He-hee!* Very well, thank you for coming in. Have a good day!"

Chapter Nine

Raskolnikov awoke in his apartment, having no memory of how he had come to be there. He tried reconstructing what might have happened. The last he remembered, he and Razumihin had been at the police station. He thought Porfiry Petrovitch was on to him, but then he wasn't, so they were leaving . . . and then nothing. It was all a blank.

"Ah, good—he's waking up," said Doctor Zossimov.

"Then he'll be all right?" asked Razumihin.

Zossimov shook his head. "It's really too soon to tell. Just make sure he gets plenty of rest and plenty to eat."

"What should we feed him?" asked Nastasya, eager to be of any assistance. "Is there anything specifically that might help?"

"What? Oh, anything, anything," replied Zossimov, "and no more medicine. I'll give him a bit now, but no more until we see if it has any positive effect, but food—he can have absolutely anything, though probably not cheese or cranberries. In fact, nothing at all that comes from a bog, but anything will do, have no worry. Oh, and no meat or fish or poultry. Just anything at all. Of course, anything but bread or gravy or banana pudding, which can be extremely aggravating to his condition."

"What exactly *is* his condition?" asked Razumihin.

"Well, I'll be honest with you, I'm not entirely certain. But I do know this—well, no, really, I have no idea," the doctor confessed.

"But surely there must be something else we can do?" said Nastasya, clutching her apron helplessly in her fists. "Is there nothing else you can tell us?"

"Uh! I almost forgot—here . . . have him take this tonic nine times per hour, and maybe try this salve—it's really for the shingles, but I don't suppose it would do any harm." Closing up his bag, Zossimov patted Raskolnikov on the shoulder. "Hang in there, my friend," the doctor said, "We'll get you back on your feet and as good as new in no time." He tipped his hat in parting, and was already out the door before poking his head back in to add, "Don't eat anything beginning with the letter 'v'. . ."

"But to eat *something* you certainly shall," said Nastasya, also heading out the door. "Maybe a lovely soup. I have some eggs. I wonder, do I have any beer?"

"Well, now," said Razumihin, pulling up a chair beside the sofa after Nastasya had gone, "finally some peace and quite, eh?"

"Yes, but . . ." Raskolnikov hesitated, nervous about asking what had happened. "I'm very confused. I wasn't . . . spinning . . . was I?"

Razumihin laughed. "No, no, of course not! Would that you had been, eh? Bit more fun, anyway, but surely you remember! Yesterday as we were leaving the police station, I'd again offered to let you help with my translations . . . to pay off your debt . . ."

None of it seemed familiar. "What did I answer?"

"Suddenly in a frenzy—right there on the steps of the police station—you grasped onto my arm and whispered something about a badger. Then you made a very wet, flatulent-like sound with your tongue, pinched me on the bottom, and fell down."

"I remember none of it."

"There, there—you're still a bit foggy. It's to be expected. And, just so you know, I'm interpreting your reply, unorthodox as it was, as a 'yes'. But for now . . ." Razumihin said, standing and returning the chair to its place along the wall, ". . . there are two visitors who are very anxious to see you." At Raskolnikov's blank stare, he added, "Your mother and sister are here!"

"Oh, dear," groaned Raskolnikov. "What a mess this all is . . ."

"And your mother is very distraught. Every time they've been by to see you, you've either been gone or unconscious."

"Well, that's a relief . . ." Raskolnikov slinked back down further under the blanket, half covering his face.

"Yes, yes, that's just what you need—rest! I'll fetch your mother and Dounia and bring them back in an hour. Until then—no trying to escape! *(Ha-ha!)* Or we'll chain you to the bed!"

And, with a wink, he was gone, leaving Raskolnikov alone.

Raskolnikov let the silence of his room settle over him. But rather than feeling any solace, he just found it eerie. Too many thoughts, questions bouncing around in his brain. What did the others know that they weren't telling him? Surely Razumihin must know—he had been there at the police station. And certainly Porfiry Petrovitch, that wily, old fox . . . and what precisely was his medical condition? Why did he keep having these attacks?

"The old woman!" he suddenly decided. "Could it be . . . remorse!? My guilty conscience rising up to bear down upon me the burden of my crime?! Oh, pish-posh!"

Raskolnikov waived his worry of conscience aside—he hadn't done anything wrong. He had been sick, it's true, before boxing Alyona Ivanovna, but that had been concerning his dilemma over whether he would claim his destiny or just go on being one of society's innumerable (and utterly dispensable) grunts. It was a psychological illness from stress and indecision and fear of reprisal, but people don't go falling down unconscious all the time from being mentally ill. If they did, the whole world would be asleep! So maybe it was the old woman herself!

"The old woman and her box!" he declared, jumping from the sofa and nearly swooning yet again. "It truly was a greasy, cruddy sort of a box . . . looked the sort to be infested, I shouldn't wonder . . . and the splinters from it! The old harpy has given me the pox!"

Pacing back and forth across his apartment, he fought to swallow back down the acidic ire rising from his gorge. "And then Raz tells me to not escape! Ha! As if I could, weak and feeble as I am, ensnared by the witch's spell. Why, I can barely stand!" He kicked at the sofa, feeling a surge of adrenaline to let go of his anger and frustration.

"Ah-ha! That's what I need—exercise! Yes, yes, that's exactly what I need! I must go for a walk immediately!"

Chapter Ten

It was a bright, warm, beautiful day and Raskolnikov wandered the streets of St. Petersburg aimlessly for hours, but the fresh air and exercise did nothing to make his thoughts and feelings any less chaotic. He was just thinking of (perhaps) finding a secluded space for a bit of spinning, but then thought better of it, instead deciding to go into a tavern and clear his head with some vodka. He found a table in the corner, hoping not to be disturbed, but no sooner had he sat down than a young man approached.

"Raskolnikov, is that you? It is!" The man grasped Raskolnikov's hand from where it had been laying on the table and shook it firmly and for far too long. "It's been ages—forever! How have you been? But you look terrible! What's happened?! Surely you remember me!" Finally releasing Raskolnikov's hand, the young man sat down, staring and feigning aghastment that he may have been forgotten.

"Oh, of course, I . . ." Flustered, Raskolnikov tried desperately to place the man. "But, no, I'm sorry I . . ."

Suddenly, the man's dejection transformed to joviality.

"*Ha!* I had you going there for half a moment, didn't I?!" Slapping his knee, he let out another loud bark of laughter. "But only half, eh? I am Dmitri Karamazov!" He extended his hand once again, which Raskolnikov hesitantly accepted.

"Karamazov!? Then Ivan—?"

"Is my brother! Or half brother, anyway. I have only just arrived back in Russia a few weeks ago," he explained, "and when I learned that Ivan was here attending university, I immediately sought him out."

"You're very close with your brother then?"

"Not at all, but I thought he might lend me money."

"I see," said Raskolnikov, though he really didn't. The serving girl stopped and Dmitri ordered a bottle of vodka for their table. When she had gone, Raskolnikov asked, "But how did you know me?"

"Ivan told me of your meeting, and the moment I saw you . . . well . . . he described a scholarly looking man, disheveled and pale—

somewhat sweaty—nearly ready for a box! When I saw you walk in I thought, 'This must be that Raskolnikov fellow! Perhaps I'll have a bit of fun with him!' And so I did!" Frowning, he became suddenly quite somber. "But I hope I have not in any way jeopardized our new friendship with my shenanigous behavior." He seemed truly quite remorseful.

"Oh, no, no, of course not. I just—*(umm)*—that is—"

"Outstanding! But I really must tell you—and don't take this badly, my friend, just because I've never known you before this very moment—but look at you! I've not laid eyes on you before, yet I can see how badly you've let yourself go!"

"I've been ill," Raskolnikov said, managing to summon a feeble smile.

"Well, I should say so! You should take better care of yourself. Ah, here she is!" The waitress deposited the bottle and two glasses and Dmitri paid her. "My treat, dear friend." He poured each of their glasses half full and raised his in salute. "To new friends! *Nastrovya!*" He downed the vodka in a gulp and Raskolnikov in turn raised his glass, but only sipped from it.

"So you say you've only just returned to Russia?"

"Indeed! I've been in America these last six years!"

Raskolnikov paled. "How dreadful . . ."

"Yes, well," Dmitri shrugged, "it was not so bad . . ." His visage abruptly darkened. "Until Grushenka, my love, ran off with a sailor who called himself 'Ishmael'! *(I still don't think he was all that he seemed . . .)*"

"There does seem a certain dire foreboding in such a name," Raskolnikov agreed.

"That's what I thought!" Dmitri declared, a smile once more breaking through his gloom.

Raskolnikov was amazed at the abruptness of the man's mood swings!

"Portents of doom and all that! Such is why I returned to Mother Russia, my homeland! And so I shall begin anew . . ." He raised his glass again in salute, but only took a small sip.

"But now! What of you, Raskolnikov, my friend? Through what dreadful straits have you passed to bring you to such unhealthy shores? What is the cause of your malady? You haven't been spending time with the ladies over to Meshchansky Street, have you?" he asked, offering a nudge and a wink.

Raskolnikov flushed at the mention of the notorious yellow-feather district of St. Petersburg. But then he suddenly thought of Sonia Semyonovna—the poor, sweet, dear thing—the touch of her hand to his cheek . . . *(the tickle of her feather on his wrist . . .!)*

"Ah-ha!" Dmitri declared, taking Raskolnikov's rising color and musing silence for confirmation of his posterior having been feathered by a woman of unclean plumage. "But, no matter, no matter, happens to the best of us . . . just that sort of a world today! Terrible things, terrible things. Why, it seems in St. Petersburg today you can barely take a step without kicking a criminal in the groin! And did you hear about that old woman who, along with her sister, had been put in a box? Happened right near here, in fact. Oh, dear! Oh, dear!"

Dmitri stood, gaping down in shock at Raskolnikov, whose color had now drained entirely from his face at the reference to Alyona Ivanovna and her sister. Raskolnikov waved away Dmitri's concern and downed the rest of his vodka.

"It's all right," Raskolnikov said, "I'm fine. It's just the illness. I feel weak sometimes yet, and—"

"Oh, well yes, of course," Dmitri agreed, reclaiming his seat. He refilled both their glasses and took a sip from his own. "But I've forgotten what I was saying."

A morbid curiosity crept over Raskolnikov. "Something about a pawnbroker woman," he said, "and her sister." Perhaps Dmitri would know the word on the street . . . if there were any suspects yet.

"Uh!" Dmitri slapped the palm of his hand against his forehead. "That's right . . . I'm such a beanhead! But at least now they've caught the fellow who did it."

"They . . . there's been an arrest?"

"Yes, just this morning. I heard they were at their wit's end on the case—no end to the list of people that would have liked to put her in a box—and she did business with so many, it seemed impossible to figure who may have been coming or going on the day it happened. Why, I myself pawned something with her just days before the incident occurred! I'll bet you've been to her as well, eh?"

"Who is this woman, you say?" Raskolnikov asked, feigning ignorance.

"Alyona Ivanovna. Surely you have heard of the old witch." Raskolnikov smiled, nodding his head slowly. "There, you see—even both of us could have been potential suspects!" Dmitri said. "*Ha-ha!* But surely not you! No one could ever expect such a thing of you, my friend."

"But what do you mean?" demanded Raskolnikov, insulted by the insinuation that he could not be capable of such an act.

"Oh, now, please, please—it's not at all a bad thing," Dmitri reassured him. "I have an eye for people, and you strike me as someone who would try to live his life by some more noble truth."

"I most certainly do!"

"Well, then how could you box two old women and think you could get away with it?" Dmitri posed the question in a condescending manner—as if to imply it should really be far too simple to have to explain. "Ach—foolishness!" he continued. "The guilt would drive you mad! You are a good man Rodion Raskolnikov, and I would bet you lead an impeccably clean life—aside from the occasional feathery illnesses, anyway." He winked conspiratorially. "But such pursuits are just necessary—they clear the mind," Dmitri said, "purge the body of ungodly lusts."

"But what if I didn't think it was a crime?" asked Raskolnikov, knowing even as he asked that perhaps he truly was mad to even tempt fate this way. "Wouldn't you say that if I were to do something that I didn't think a crime—indeed something I perhaps thought would benefit others—I should have no cause to feel guilty?"

"Well, yes, certainly, but—"

"And you say you've done business with the woman? Then you know what a harpy she was, yes?"

"Yes, but . . . well . . . certainly—"

"So perhaps it was I, after all, who did society this favor, sacrificing the unwanted who drag the rest down in favor of the many—to raise the common whole to greater heights of good!"

Fear blazed in Dmitri's eyes, as they stared at one another over the table in silence for several minutes, each filled with thoughts and speculations and doubt. Suddenly Dmitri's eyes broke away and he laughed loudly.

"*Ha!* And now you've almost had me!" he said, banging his fist on the table. "You devil, you! But I've only just said they have the culprit in custody! Well, I'm glad to see that your illness hasn't affected your wit any."

Raskolnikov shook his head, trying to free his thoughts from the fog of anger and superiority that filled his brain. "But you haven't said—who have they arrested? How did they catch the scoundrel?"

"He gave himself up. It was one of the painters who had been working in another apartment who has been fingered."

"Oh, my!"

"Well, figuratively speaking."

"Oh, yes, well I see."

"You don't seem at all relieved to know the criminal isn't still loose," commented Dmitri.

Relieved?! thought Raskolnikov, swimming in a tumultuous sea of conflicting emotions. *To know an innocent man has been captured in my stead!?*

Raskolnikov quickly excused himself, apologizing for having to run off, but claiming he was sick again and wanted to return home before losing consciousness. When he was well out of sight of the tavern and Dmitri, should he be watching, Raskolnikov doubled back and headed for Alyona Ivanovna's apartment. He felt consumed with a fervorous red rage, almost not even in control of his own actions, but merely watching, as if just slightly removed and following helplessly along behind himself.

He leapt up the four flights of stairs, taking three at a time, and despite his illness he was not breathing any harder than normal when he reached the top. The door to the apartment was slightly open; he pushed it the rest of the way, knowing at any moment the box would come into view, but it was gone! He walked in slowly, oblivious to the workmen there refurbishing and preparing for a new tenant. There was a spot on the floor where the box had been, all red and sticky, as if someone—it seemed to Raskolnikov—had perhaps spilled a bowl of Jell-O or something, and it had melted into the carpet.

"Hey, you can't be here," said the workers' foreman, gaining Raskolnikov's attention with a tug at his sleeve. "If you've got something to pawn . . ."

"Where is it?" Raskolnikov interrupted.

"Where is what?"

"The old woman and her box?"

The foreman warily took a step back, his eyes drawn to the side . . . to a closet . . . its door open . . . and the box. Raskolnikov stared at the box for a moment, his rage ebbing, focus returning.

"Look," said the foreman, "if you have something to pawn, you'll have to take it elsewhere. We've got work to do and don't need you getting in our way."

Continuing to stare at the box for a moment, Raskolnikov realized it had been a mistake to have come here. Finally returning his attention to the foreman, he indicated the spot on the floor and commented, "That's a bloody mess!"

And he turned, darted out the door, flew down the stairs and ran all the way home.

Chapter Eleven

Upon entering his room, Raskolnikov felt an involuntary shudder of déjà vu. Once again, having come from *that apartment*, he found a congregation of people waiting for him at his own apartment. The moment he walked in the door, all present leapt to their feet and stared at him in amazement.

"Oh, thank heavens!" cried his mother, rushing forward to embrace him.

"We were all very worried, Rodya," his sister Dounia added, offering a sisterly punch in the neck.

Ignoring them both, Raskolnikov's eyes lit up feverishly. Pulling away from his mother, he ran to Razumihin, who had once again sat down on the chair by the door. Looming over him, flushed and dripping sweat from running, Raskolnikov scuffled his hair and chanted, "Raz-Raz-Razumihin—*Razimataz!!*"

"He's mad!" declared Dr. Zossimov, stepping forward even as he seemed not to want to get too close. "Mad, I tell you! Positively deranged! Quickly restrain him—or fetch a brick!"

With a sharp bark of a laugh, Raskolnikov plopped down onto the sofa, amused by the looks of near panic on all those around him. "I'm no madder than an infested and feral tree monkey on opium!"

"*A brick, I say!* To bludgeon him back to sanity!"

"Good doctor, I assure you, I'm perfectly well. As healthy as a horse!"

"Yes, well, I've seen some pretty sick horses."

"Oh, don't you all see," Razumihin chimed in at last, "he's just having a bit of fun at our expense, eh Rodya? It only goes to show he's getting back to his old self."

"Well, even so, you shouldn't have worried us by going out again so soon," commented his mother, but she seemed relieved by Razumihin's explanation.

"Yes, yes," replied Raskolnikov, waving away her concern. "But what if I were mad? Truly, aren't all of us our own breed of madman? Each with his own particular penchant or peculiar panache?"

"Alliteration!" cried Zossimov. "A brick—or even a very stout log!"

"What I mean is," continued Raskolnikov, paying no mind to the doctor's frenzied outburst, "if you were to call me mad, wouldn't you be judging my madness from the *presumed* vantage of your own sanity?"

"Yes, I suppose you're right," agreed Razumihin, stroking his chin philosophically, "but what if you're just an idiot? And, anyway, what is your obsession with madness lately? You were going on about it with Ivan Karamazov just the other day as well."

"I wouldn't call it an obsession," Raskolnikov replied defensively.

"Well, an incessant preoccupation then, eh?"

"Oh, all this blather!" declared Pulcheria. "For the time being, let's act on the presumption that we're all sane—unless someone starts foaming at the mouth or something—and since you're feeling better Rodya, we do have certain family matters to discuss." She turned to Zossimov and Razumihin. "If you don't mind, gentlemen . . ."

"No, wait," said Raskolnikov, "not Raz…Raz can stay. Through . . . my illness . . . , he's been an absolute brick!"

"Ah-ha!" Doctor Zossimov shouted in triumph, but then seeing he was yet to be ignored, he wandered meekly out of the apartment.

"Yes, of course," agreed Dounia, and blushed faintly. "Of course your friend may stay. It's clear, the two of you seem almost like brothers."

Razumihin offered a slight bow of thanks to her, Raskolnikov noting a slight coloring in his complexion as well.

Hookie, who's got the cookie? he thought to himself.

"Now, Rodya," began his mother, "we've had some disturbing news from your sister's betrothed, Mr. Luzhin."

"Yes, what's it all about?" demanded Dounia. "Pyotr Petrovitch said that you were very rude—that you threatened him even. I hope it was only the delirium from your illness at work."

"You must understand," added Pulcheria, "all the trouble to which Mrs. Svidrigailov went to arrange this match."

"Svidrigailov!" Raskolnikov jumped to his feet. "Luzhin can wait—though I must tell you straight out I don't like him—but you should know that Svidrigailov is in Petersburg!"

"But, whatever for? Surely he didn't follow after me?!"

"No, Dounia—or, at any rate, such is what he purports—he came with money. His wife, well, she had to be put into a box . . .."

"Oh, the poor woman!" said Pulcheria, shaking her head sadly.

"She left you three thousand rubles in her will," continued Raskolnikov. "And, in addition, for the trouble he caused you, he said he was giving you an additional *ten* thousand!"

Razumihin whistled.

"What did you tell him?" Dounia asked, clearly perplexed by the matter.

"I told him I didn't think you would accept the money, but I would at least inform you it was offered."

"It is a great deal of money to refuse," pointed out his mother.

"But what goes along with it, I wonder . . .." mused Dounia.

"I beg your pardon," interjected Razumihin. "I don't mean to speak out of place here, but this could be the answer for all of us!"

"How do you mean?" asked Raskolnikov.

"We could start our own publishing company! All three of us, translating texts into Russian, and even publishing our own Russian writers."

"But it would be Dounia's money . . .."

"Oh, of course, of course," Razumihin quickly agreed. But what was it Mussorgski always used to say? Uh!—how does that go now...does anyone have an orchestra handy? . . . no? . . . oh, bother! Well, perhaps it wasn't so much after all."

"What are you going on about?!" Raskolnikov was feeling less 'mad' by the minute and beginning to wonder about his dear friend Razumihin.

"No, he's right," said Dounia. "It would be perfect. Of course we'd have to work out all the details, but—" She looked boldly into Razumihin's face, her eyes glistening brightly. "Well . . . then I wouldn't have to marry Pyotr Petrovitch."

"So you truly were marrying him simply for financial security!" said Raskolnikov, his ire rising.

"Oh, don't pontificate to me, brother," she replied tersely. "You would have done the same if you had found yourself in my circumstances."

"I would *never*," he declared vehemently, "marry that man!"

"We can count our blessings on that account anyway," commented Pulcheria, fanning herself and rolling her eyes. "But it seems it doesn't have to be an issue now. I suggest, as it is getting late and Rodya should get his rest, that we all sleep on the idea and when we meet tomorrow we can discuss it with a fresh outlook."

"A wise course, indeed," agreed Razumihin. "We can meet again tomorrow—perhaps for lunch?"

They took their leave, Razumihin offering to escort Pulcheria and Dounia back to their lodgings, and Raskolnikov was at last alone.

Slumping back into the sofa, he muttered to himself, "A bloody mess indeed . . ."

Chapter Twelve

The strangely chaotic euphoria Raskolnikov had felt leaving Alyona Ivanovna's apartment had now entirely ebbed, leaving him thoroughly depleted. So much so, he failed to hear the light tap on the door or the subtle creak as it was slowly opened . . .

"Returned from the scene of the crime, eh?"

Raskolnikov started, his feverishly muddled thoughts banished as he looked up to see Porfiry Petrovich standing in the doorway. His heart thundered in his chest under the dark glare of the police constable. The man's words sank in and Raskolnikov now felt it was all he could do to gulp his heart back down out of his throat!

"Constable Petrovich," he squeaked. "I—that is—the scene—? I beg your pardon!"

The constable's stern composure abruptly broke. "*He-hee!* Oh, you must call me Porfiry, I insist. May I?" The constable gestured to invite permission to enter, to which, after the slightest hesitation, Raskolnikov nodded his acquiescence. Porfiry entered, about to sit on the broken chair, but noting its instability chose another instead. "Well, I hope you were not offended by my 'scene of the crime' comment? Merely in jest, I assure you—*he-hee!* A little police humor, you see. I was in the neighborhood and thought to stop by and see how you were recovering. It's not an inconvenient time, I trust?"

"Oh—no, no, not at all," Raskolnikov replied, trying to retain his composure. "I mean, yes!" Raskolnikov abruptly stood, causing Porfiry Petrovich to follow suit. "Actually, I was just about to go out for a while and—"

"Really?" said Porfiry, sitting back down and scratching his temple thoughtfully. "Of course—and perhaps I am mistaken, eh?—but it was to my understanding that you had only just returned home."

How did he know that!? Raskolnikov wondered to himself. *Is he having me watched?!*

"Uh, yes, yes, that is correct," he said aloud. "But only . . . to see my mother and sister, who have just gone, you see, and now—"

"Ah, yes, I saw them leaving as I came in—*he-hee-hee!*" The constable smirked and winked. "Hookie-hookie, who's got the cookie, eh?"

Raskolnikov's blood ran cold. *What he himself had said . . .?!* Surely it must be the return of his delirium—a relapse of his illness due to the stress of the moment. Raskolnikov slumped back into the sofa and hugged his blankie. "Um . . . yes . . ."

"Oh, forgive me, please, my friend," Porfiry begged. "I only just meant I could see how your sister and that friend of yours . . ."

"Razumihin," Raskolnikov offered.

"Razumihin! I only meant I could see how they looked at one another."

"No, no," Raskolnikov waved away further explanation. "You're—I think you're right, they seem quite fond of one another."

"Yes!—*he-hee!*—yes, that is truly all I meant." Porfiry cleared his throat. "Forgive my asking, Rodya, but you wouldn't happen to have a spot of vodka, would you? I had dinner just before stopping here, and there's nothing better than a spot of vodka after a lovely meal of smoked fish and jam! I— Oh! Dear man!" Porfiry was set aback by Raskolnikov, who had turned white as a ghost, clutching even tighter to the blankie.

"Smoked fish?" he managed to squeak. "And . . . *jam* . . ."

"That's right," Porfiry agreed. "You know, you look as if you could do with a spot of vodka, as well, eh? *He-hee!*"

He's toying with me! Raskolnikov screamed in his head. *Trying to make me crack! But how does he seem to know my own inner thoughts?! Unless he's God or something! Oh, my G—I mean . . . holy crud! He's God!! He can probably hear what I'm thinking, even now! I'd better—"*

Porfiry sat calmly, merely gazing at Raskolnikov's discomfiture. Raskolnikov tried to close his mind from any thought with an endless mantra of *La-la-la-la-la-la-la~!!*

"You know, my friend," the constable said, "although at the moment you are quite twitchy and, well . . . rather odd I must say . . . since our first meeting, you have struck me as a man of destiny . . . do you understand? A man who can appreciate striving toward the greater good for all, eh? Not afraid to break a few eggs, as it were, to make an omelet—"

"Well, good, good!" Raskolnikov was on his feet, verily leaping across the room to open the door. *Why?! Why?! Why?! Why?! If he isn't God, why doesn't he just arrest me? And if He is—why won't He just smite me down!?* Turning back to the startled constable, he grinned much too largely and said, "Good of you to stop in, Const—I mean, Porfiry. Sorry to be so abrupt, but I truly must get going, as . . . ah, I'm meeting someone!"

"Oh, yes, of course, of course! *He-hee!* I didn't mean to detain you." Porfiry offered half a bow and, putting on his hat, turned to leave. "I shall wish you a good evening then and—oh!"

"Oh?" *So close!*

"Well, I just wondered . . . about my query when I first arrived?" said Porfiry, with a shrug. "Simply for curiosity's sake, of course . . ."

"Your query?"

"Yes, you remember, my quip about 'returning from the scene of the crime'? What business, precisely, took you to such an inauspicious locale?"

"Ah, yes, well . . ." Raskolnikov's mind was a total blank and he and Porfiry Petrovich stared at one another for fully nine minutes in silence—or so it seemed to Raskolnikov, though it was, in truth, closer to nine seconds—before inspiration struck.

"I was looking for a job!" Raskolnikov declared triumphantly. He felt like sticking his hand in his jacket like Napoleon, but, as he wasn't wearing one, he thought it might look silly. "The painters? On the flat below . . . the pawnbroker's apartment?"

"Ah, yes, I see, I see," Porfiry replied, nodding appreciatively, beginning to pace back and forth as if in deep contemplation. "Of course, you refer to the arrest that has been made in the case?"

"That's right—I thought they might be hiring, you see, and I do after all have that promissory note to pay off to my landlady . . ."

Porfiry stopped his pacing and leaned in toward Raskolnikov, speaking conspiratorially, though they were the only two people in the room, saying, "You know, I believe—and it is only a hunch, mind you *(he-hee!)*—that we may not have the right man in custody . . ."

Before Raskolnikov could respond, the constable offered a wink and a tip of his hat and he was out the door.

Chapter Thirteen

Raskolnikov listened as the sound of Porfiry Petrovich's footsteps faded down the stairs, relishing the silence that followed their departure.

Gone! he thought, yet his sense of relief was short-lived. Or *is **He**?! If Porfiry is God, is He not . . . everywhere!?*

Wishing to either have a violently rigorous spin—though his head and heart felt as though he had already done so—or just curl up under his blankie, tucked away safe on his couch forever, Raskolnikov knew neither was viable. On the off chance the constable was *not* the Almighty, but might be following him, or at any rate having him followed, Raskolnikov had to go through with his façade of being late for an appointment.

Thus, unsure of where even to go, Raskolnikov again headed out into the St. Petersburg night. Yet barely down the front steps to the sidewalk, he spied Razumihin coming his way. A notion flashed in his mind and without a second thought he decided to act upon it.

"Raz! Razumihin!!" he called, waving wildly at his friend, though by this time Razumihin was only a few feet away. "It is I! Rodya Raskolnikov!"

"Ah-ha!" exclaimed Razumihin, clutching Raskolnikov firmly by the shoulders, half embrace, half-placating restraint. "Trying again to escape, eh? Well, you'll not get by me! Just where do you think you're off to now, after I so persuasively reassured your mother that I would keep you under wraps?"

"Oh, no, no, it's not like that," Raskolnikov replied, brushing free from Razumihin's grasp. "I just needed a bit of air (maybe a nip of vodka) and then off to bed—I promise! But since I've run into you, there's a . . . a favor I wanted to ask of you."

"Anything, my friend—whatever is in my power to give is yours!"

"That's good to know because it is really so very important. You see, I was wondering, if something should happen to me . . ."

Razumihin frowned. "What could happen?! Look at you, almost completely recovered!"

"I didn't necessarily mean my illness," Raskolnikov confessed. "But, well yes, let's say for argument's sake I were to have a relapse and had to go away for a while—to the hospital. Would you mind . . . I mean . . ."

"Rodya! I've never seen you so bashful! Come on then, out with it."

"Could you possibly look after my mother and Dounia? *If* anything were to happen . . ."

Razumihin took an involuntary step back as if he'd been struck, his jaw dropping open speechlessly. "Oh, Rodya Raskolnikov . . . you honor me beyond my greatest expectations!"

"Oh, pish-posh. I see how you are with Dounia, and I would trust my mother's well-being with no one so much as with you."

"But, I am *unworthy*," Razumihin protested. "I . . . I am a dog! A scabby little mongrel oozing pus onto her dress, leaving poo in her shoe—only so I might guiltily lick her lovely hands to show how very sorry I am!"

Raskolnikov dug his hands into his pockets and shrugged, rolling his eyes. "Well, I think that might be a bit . . . *dramatic* . . ."

"Nuzzle my muzzle to her groin to make amends," Razumihin continued, panting heavily, his face in a sneer. "And then I'd take my filthy paws to her and—"

"Enough, my friend! You are too hard on yourself. They could have no better protector than you. And I know that mother would approve."

"Oh, well, yes," said Razumihin, his fervorous self-abasement of a moment ago entirely vanished. "I didn't mean I wouldn't look after your mom—moms are easy, just tell them what you know they want to hear, but then go about your business as you like anyway. But Dounia!?"

Resting a calming hand on Razumihin's shoulder, Raskolnikov said, "I know she cares for you, too, Raz. I can see it in how she looks at you."

"But I am a dog!"

"Yes, yes, I remember," Raskolnikov cut him off, "but . . . well . . . she always wanted a puppy. Anyway, I must run. I'm late for an appointment! We can discuss this further tomorrow; just think on it, all right?"

He turned and began down the street, and Razumihin was frazzled enough he did not think to stop him or ask about any appointments, for which Raskolnikov was infinitely grateful. Upon getting to the pub, Raskolnikov decided his head was clear enough he didn't need any vodka. His thoughts seemed clearer now than they had since . . . since the night he boxed Alyona Ivanovna. The thought did not settle well with him and he passed by the pub and headed toward the park for a raucous bout of spinning. A clear head was the last thing he needed just then!

Rounding the corner, he was nearly bowled over—and nearly bowled over in turn—a young man bustling along in the opposite direction.

"Oh! Pardon me!" the man exclaimed, steadying Raskolnikov as if he might still spill over. "I am so dreadfully sorry—walking along, head in a book when I should watch where I'm going."

"Not at all," Raskolnikov replied, wishing to simply rush past and get on to the park. "No harm done, I—"

His eye caught the name of the author of the article the man was reading: Rodion R. Raskolnikov.

"What's that?!" he demanded.

"What, this?" replied the man, taken aback by Raskolnikov's vehemence. "It—it's just an article about crime and Napoleon and . . . and, well, about God, I suppose."

"But that's my article!"

"You are Rodion R. Raskolnikov?!"

"I am and I wrote that article, but they never said they were going to print it—that had to have been six months ago!"

"Well, I don't know what to tell you." The man shrugged, holding the magazine out to Raskolnikov. "But here it is! I'm sorry, I'm being quite rude. My name is Alyosha Karamazov," he said, holding his hand out to Raskolnikov.

"*Another* Karamazov!?" Raskolnikov replied, shaking Alyosha's hand. "You guys are just *everywhere* . . ."

"You've met other Karamazovs then?"

"Yes, an Ivan and a Dmitri—do you know them?"

"Ah, yes…" Alyosha frowned. "Yes, those are indeed of my Karamazovs…but as I'd been about to say—with regard to your article—I was greatly intrigued by your rationalization of Napoleon; justified as it were in his actions, in that he was an 'exceptional' individual concerned with the greater good for all . . ."

Raskolnikov paled at the mention of "the greater good" yet again, recalling his very unsettling conversation with Porfiry Petrovich. Glancing nervously all about—simply positive he was being watched—he replied in a nervously high-pitched voice, "Oh, really!? How interesting! And what was your take on all that?"

"Well!" Alyosha replied, aghast. "It's preposterous! To think that there could be individuals above the laws and the necessary societal traditions and boundaries that keep us all in check! And, further, that this would be deemed aligned with God's plan!?"

Raskolnikov took an involuntary step back. "God!?!"

Could this be who was tailing him?! Dubiously, he dismissed the notion; if Porfiry Petrovich were indeed the Almighty, He would not need a human spy.

"Yes, God," Alyosha continued. "You see, what I find so alarming about it all is that we are, each of us, responsible for everyone else—in the most basic sense, stemming all the way back to Original Sin. No man stands above, and certainly not such men as Napoleon or Caesar, and others of the like *(the devils!)*"

Raskolnikov felt as if a shard of ice had pierced him—straight through the heart and into his very soul. "Each . . . responsible . . . for all?"

"But of course!" Alyosha seemed pleased to have caused a reaction. "Else how could it all work? It would be chaos! That is the supernal beauty and brilliance of God's plan."

Raskolnikov's world felt undone. *Could it be true?! How could I have been so blind! But—no—it's just his theory! (And who the hell is he?!) I'll have to work it out.*

"You know," began Alyosha, interrupting Raskolnikov's silent speculations, "it somehow reminds me of what St. John said: 'Verily, verily, do I say unto thee, except a corn of wheat falls into the ground, it abideth alone: yet if it be done, it bringeth forth much fruit'!"

Raskolnikov frowned. "But, whatever can it mean?!"

"I don't know," replied Alyosha in really quite a smarmy fashion. "I just don't know, but it always makes me hungry. Would you care to join me? For—oh, I don't know—some corn or some wheat or some fruit or something? Maybe a taco?"

"Thank you, Alyosha, but . . . tacos?" Raskolnikov shook it off. "No! No, I thank you, but there is someone I really must see most urgently!"

"Another time then" Alyosha offered with a bow. "It has been a pleasure to have met you, Rodion Raskolnikov."

"And you," Raskolnikov mumbled automatically, already turning to leave. "You have given me a great deal to consider . . ."

Chapter Fourteen

Raskolnikov verily ran to Sonia Semyonovna's apartment—yet so great was his inner turmoil, he could not begin to think what he would say to her. *Do I just wish to know her view of God's plan,* he wondered, or . . . *shall I confess all to her!?*

His trepidation—if not outright fear—caused him to take a somewhat circuitous route to her apartment, yet circling ever nearer. When he at last arrived, steeling himself to rap lightly on the door, he was disappointed (and relieved!) to find her not at home.

"Well, then that's that!" he declared, pounding his fist into the opposite palm. About to head for his own apartment, he hesitated. "All right, I'll just try the door; if it's locked I'll go, and if it's open—"

The door swung slowly open as he turned the handle, revealing the dark, drear interior.

"Bugger! Then I suppose I'll wait."

After lighting the lamp on the table beside the door, he sat on the edge of the bed—until he realized it was a *feather* bed (with a yellow coverlet!), and recalling her profession, he became really quite giddy and decided he would stand.

"I should never have come," he muttered, beginning to pace. "Why should this Alyosha Karamazov get me in such a quandary? What does he know?! It's just his opinion next to my own, after all. It's not as if he had some inside information—not as if he were in a monastery or anything *(though he did rather smell somehow . . . monkish).* But what am I about here? Surely I can't confess all to Sonia! What would she think of me?! To know I had stuffed an old woman (and her sister) into a box for a few baubles. No—no, it was for the greater good! *(Unless you're Alyosha*

Karamazov—with his 'Original Sin'!) It's not too late—I can just go and she'll have never known—"

Raskolnikov's rant ended abruptly as he became acutely aware of someone standing in the doorway. It took half a moment for him to recognize—it was Svidrigailov.

"We meet again, Rodion Raskolnikov," Svidrigailov greeted him, as he entered the apartment toting a large wooden box along behind him.

"What are you doing here?" Raskolnikov demanded. "I thought you were leaving the country . . . or something."

"Yes, well . . ." Svidrigailov threw his hands in the air and rolled his eyes, casually sitting on the box. "The 'or something' has taken precedence—though I think new options are opening up for me."

"Meaning what, exactly?"

"I never would have taken you for a fan of pugilism—though I understand you've taken up *boxing* . . ." Noting the sudden intensity of Raskolnikov's gaze, Svidrigailov bid a hasty verbal retreat. "Now, now, my friend, let's remain civil. I happen to let the apartment next door, you see, and the walls are so thin—I couldn't help but overhear you talking to yourself."

"What do you want?"

"I merely wish to propose a deal. You see what straits I've come to, eh?" He, almost lovingly, stroked his box. "But, given recent insights, rather than putting myself in a box, I would like to ask for your sister Dounia's hand."

"You sick bastard!" Raskolnikov ejaculated. "And what of the rest of her?!"

"Well, it is after all attached, and I'm sure with your brotherly guidance you could persuade her to consider me as a suitor—the 'whole' of her, of course."

Raskolnikov's dread at the prospect of confessing to Sonia had now become a cold, dark abyss in his soul—the fate of his sister directly influenced by his crime *(not that it was a crime,* he reminded himself, *though then why do I feel a need to confess anything?!)*.

"All right," Svidrigailov said, standing and walking toward the door—but leaving the box behind. "I see I've given you much to think upon. We shall speak again soon."

After Svidrigailov had gone, Raskolnikov resumed frantically pacing, contemplating what next to do. Should he still tell Sonia what he'd done? Did it even matter at this point whether or not God intended the greater good or for each to be responsible for all? As his pacing became ever more frantic, his mind agog, thoughts swirling madly out of control, Raskolnikov barely even realized he'd begun to spin—whirling and twirling, faster and faster, the apartment a hazy blur, his entire existence but a hazy blur . . . until he caught his foot in the yellow bedspread and tripped, falling head-first into the side of Svidrigailov's abandoned box and . . .

Chapter Fifteen

Raskolnikov awoke in darkness, confined in a cramped wooden cube. Svidrigailov's box! *Had the fiend come back and put him in a box?!* Perhaps he could get the lid open—he'd heard about others who had come back from the box, if they had only very recently been boxed and the lid had not been entirely secured.

He reached up and gasped in shock as his hand passed through the wood, as though through air! He instinctively sought to pull back, but something without grabbed him and pulled. Suddenly Raskolnikov found himself hurled out of the box—straight through the seemingly solid lid—being held in tow by someone. The pair flew straight up, passing through the ceiling of Sonia's apartment, high into the sky. As they soared through the clouds he almost thought they looked like a giant, white, puffy Porfiry Petrovich, the eyes flashing with lightning, thunder rumbling *"HE-HEE-HEE!!!"*, but then in only half a moment they were through, and he silently admonished himself, thinking, *Don't be ridiculous, man! Only your imagination.*

Now racing beyond the very Earth itself, the pair flew through space, their speed increasing each second as they soared past the planets and moons and asteroids and comets. Soon they were beyond the solar system, immersed in the cold, inky void of interstellar space.

"Well!" commented Raskolnikov, as the initial shock of the experience began to fade, "this sort of beats the hell out of spinning, eh?"

His guide glanced back and frowned. "I be Smerdyakov."

Taking his first truly close look at the man, Raskolnikov was startled to note he looked like a badger! *(And, oddly enough, a bit like a Karamazov . . .)*

"I'm Raskolnikov."

"I know you."

"Hey, are those horns?" He'd just then noticed two rather bovine protrusions on Smerdyakov's head.

"More or less...proper horns be bone; these be more an . . . teeth."

"You have giant teeth jutting out of the top of your skull?!"

Smerdyakov shrugged.

"Freaky!"

"Not nearly—ere the Nether Realm . . ."

"You're from Amsterdam then!"

"Nether *Realm*, not Nether*lands* . . . I be denizen'd of Hell!"

"Oh...and so then is that where you're taking me?"

Again, Smerdyakov shrugged. Raskolnikov thought his question would go unanswered, but then Smerdyakov replied, "Not as you might expect."

They flew on in silence. Raskolnikov had no concept of time—minutes, hours, days, all were conceivable to him—as they hurtled through the void, the distant stars but streaming streaks of light. And then he was suddenly roused from the trance he had fallen into. They were decelerating into a new star system, and before long Raskolnikov noted the planet they were approaching.

Flying through the sky, Raskolnikov basked in the beauty of this wild, untamed world—the forests and rivers and mountains and oceans, the teeming wildlife running and flying and swimming in unchecked abundance.

"But, can it be?!" Raskolnikov whispered, as realization crept over him. "The Earth?! But how?"

"It be, indeed, *an* Earth," Smerdyakov replied. "Though not of yours, for this Earth hath been not tarnished by the Fall of Man."

Eden itself! Raskolnikov thought, and about to ask where all the people were, they landed in the midst of a tribe of seemingly primitive humans.

"Your fate now be your own," Smerdyakov said as he released his hold on Raskolnikov. Without another word, he vanished in a fetid puff of smoke.

The people of this Earth initially seemed as curious about Raskolnikov as he was about them. What surprised him was how quickly their interest waned—after only the briefest of perusals of his person, they seemed contented with his presence, simply accepting him as one of their own. He discovered they were indeed primitive, in that there was no civilization—no sense of society or even a tribal affiliation; everyone simply came and went as they chose, even the children, who were cared for and loved by all. They lived *with* the world, not *from* it . . . alongside even what would have been the most ferocious of wild animals on his own Earth, and in tune with all of nature. Most of all Raskolnikov was struck by how every one them, at every moment, looked as if he or she had just had a good, rugged spin! But he knew they had not . . . there was no need here for spinning.

After he had been there for a time—he knew not whether it had been days or weeks or even months—his curiosity could be restrained no longer and he approached one who had helped initiate Raskolnikov to this strange new world.

"Nagoi," he said, "how is it that there seems to be no crime here? Everyone seems so contented—and yet no one has anything!"

Nagoi laughed.

"But we have everything!" he said, gesturing to the whole wide world around him. "But what is this . . . 'crime' of which you ask?"

"Well, I mean . . . wrong-doing . . . doing things to hurt others for one's own benefit," Raskolnikov explained. "There seems to be no conception of good or evil here; everything simply . . . *IS* . . ."

Shaking his head, Nagoi replied, "You speak in riddles I cannot fathom. Naturally, everything *IS* . . . for if something *ISN'T*, well, I suppose we just wouldn't even know about it! But I do not understand why one might purposely cause harm to another; we are each responsible for all."

The very words of Alyosha Karamazov! Raskolnikov thought, taken aback to hear this same concept in a world untarnished by the Fall.

"It is of no benefit," Nagoi continued, "to seek for one's self at the expense of another, for such would cause hardship to all."

Raskolnikov could not get his mind around such a selfless concept—though Nagoi's words did seem reflective of Raskolnikov's own theory of seeking the greater good. But where was the greed? Where was the animosity and violence that marked the society on his own Earth? There was no theft here—since no one possessed anything of their own—and there was no yellow feathering or untimely boxing of others. Indeed, if they hadn't known how to distill vodka, the only apparent science they had, he wouldn't have even believed them to be human!

"Well, it's a bit different in my world," said Raskolnikov, truly hoping to glean some understanding, as well as to have Nagoi understand his own perspective. "There people *have* things, you see. For example, you have a home, a dwelling of some sort, where you can be sheltered from the weather or from the malice of others, and where you can keep a lot of your other possessions."

"What sorts of possessions?" Nagoi asked. Others in the area were beginning to gather around.

"Oh, all sorts of things . . . books, for example." He then spent much too long trying to explain to these people who lacked a written language what a book was. "All right, okay, forget about books. Let's say you have a really fun time playing a game one day, and then on the same day you find a pretty rock that you like and wish to keep as a memento of that day. Do you see?"

"There are many pretty rocks . . ." Nagoi said.

"Ah, yes, but this is the prettiest rock you've ever seen, and you want to keep it with you always—cherish it. But then someone else sees this rock that you have and he wants it, too! For it is the prettiest rock *he* has ever seen . . . and so he takes it!"

"But . . . if he wants the rock, I would gladly give it to him. There is no need to take it from me . . ."

"Okay, but let's say that there are only just so many really pretty rocks available, certainly not enough for everyone to have one. So if you want to have a pretty rock, you can't take them and just go giving your rocks off to everybody!"

His outburst was met with a stunned silence—interrupted by a young girl's giggle in the back of the throng that had assembled. She waggled a peacock feather at him and winked.

"Moving on . . ." he continued. "So perhaps someone covets your pretty rock, but you don't want to give it to him, so he tries to take it! And so you struggle, but in the end he knocks you to the ground, grabs the rock and runs away! What about that?"

He saw a few people in the crowd nodding their heads in understanding.

"That must be a *very* pretty rock . . ." someone commented.

Nagoi still seemed unable to grasp what Raskolnikov was getting at, but then a gleam of understanding alit in his eyes. "Or, perhaps," he ventured, "someone might have a good, stout stick that I admired?"

"Exactly!"

"And so on your world, I would just knock him down and take it!"

"Um . . ." Raskolnikov floundered, realizing his error. "Well, no— ideally not. You see, we have something called money." His explanation of money and finance, going about as successfully as had his explanation of books, Raskolnikov again brought it down to a more basic level. "Bartering, then, is when someone has for example several pretty rocks, and they want to trade them for something that someone else has—such as a good, stout stick."

"Or a seashell?"

"Yes! Exactly! Whatever might be of value to both parties, and then they just trade their goods in a quantity that they feel is fair and acceptable to both."

"What if it isn't acceptable to both parties?" someone called out.

"Then you knock him down!" Nagoi cried, fire in his eyes. "And you take it!!"

Without warning, the crowd erupted into chaos, everyone yelling and darting all about, gathering up all the pretty rocks and stout sticks and seashells they could find, hoarding them and building great cities with dwellings where they could protect their possessions. Governments were formed and scientific technology triumphed over nature. Wars were fought— and boxes were made—boxes beyond imagining, yet ever needing more, never enough for the need of them. People began spinning—and why not? Their entire civilization was already spinning completely out of control!

My fault . . . Raskolnikov knew. *And it's ALL my fault. I am the Forbidden Fruit of this Earth—and they hath eaten of me! (Hell, I veritably crammed it down their throats!) Slurping down all the depraved juices of my being!*

He went to see Nagoi, who had become the tyrant who ruled over the people. Nagoi, much to Raskolnikov's uneasiness, dressed now really rather like Napoleon. He even had his right hand tucked into the breast of his coat. Before he noticed Raskolnikov approaching, Nagoi pulled a small badger out of his breast pocket, whispered something to it, bestowed several affectionate little kissies and then returned it to its hiding place.

"Nagoi," said Raskolnikov, "I must beg your forgiveness! I have let evil into your world and I was wrong to do it—never meant to do it! You must try to make things as they were—restore peace and order."

"No, no, my friend," Nagoi replied with a big, phony, French accent, "you have given us wisdom, which has brought us science and law, the insight to strive toward the greater good for the many—and we now *own* this world! And it is only in doing so that we may one day find true happiness!"

"But don't you see?" Raskolnikov pleaded. "You already *had* your happiness! And I destroyed it—don't let me be your destroyer!"

Nagoi cast him off.

"Bah! I have no time for this drivel! Let's go for a spin, shall we? *Weeeeeeeee!*" And he grabbed Raskolnikov tightly and they whirled and twirled all away—until Nagoi lost his grasp and Raskolnikov went hurtling head-first into a tree.

Chapter Sixteen

Raskolnikov again awoke in darkness—expecting to either find himself bloodied under a tree or in Svidrigailov's box. Instead, he was sprawled out next to the box (and only slightly bloodied) with Sonia Semyonovna leaning over him, seeming extremely vexed.

"Rodya?" she said, helping him to sit up. "What are you doing here? Are you okay? What . . . is this your . . . what is the box for?"

"Sonia!" Raskolnikov replied. "I'm sorry . . . to have you find me here like this. I didn't know who else I could turn to."

"But of course, you can come to me for anything."

"Thank you, Sonia, but you may change your mind after what I have to say."

Getting up, he led her to the bed and sat her down on the edge. Pacing back and forth before her—unable to look her in the eye—he began his confession.

"You see, Sonia, I've done something that—I think (perhaps)—I really ought not to have done. I've been ill, as you know, and it may have skewed my thinking on a matter or two."

"Rodya, please—we all do things we wish we hadn't. Sometimes there is no choice in the matter, but there is nothing that can be done that cannot be *un*done."

"Yes, yes, I agree, but . . ."

Bracing himself, he blurted out, "It was I who put the old pawnbroker and her sister into a box!"

"Oh!" Sonia sat in quiet stun for a moment—the silence screaming in Raskolnikov's soul. "*That,*" she said, "*can't* be undone . . ."

"I know!" he cried, falling at her feet and laying his head in her lap. "I know, and now I don't know what to do. Turn myself into the police? Run away? Pretend it didn't happen? I just don't know."

"Why, Rodya—why did you do it?"

"She was a vile old harpy and I thought I was doing the world a favor to rid it of her. I thought . . . well, I truly thought it would be to the greater good of us all."

"What sort of a world would it be if we were, each of us, all going to assume for ourselves what that greater good should be?" said Sonia, lifting his face to look her in the eye. "We are all but brothers and sisters, all the children of God, and each must be responsible for all."

"Yes, yes, I get that *now,*" replied Raskolnikov, exasperated. "But you see, in a way, it wasn't the old woman at all who I put into a box—but myself. For such is my life now, locked away by my secret crime."

"But yours is only a *figurative* box . . ."

"Well, yes, that is true."

"And you *literally* put those two women into a truly very real box."

"All right! Yes, I *literally* put them in a box—and I am *sorry.* I must face my punishment and try to make amends."

Sonia gingerly stood and stepped around him, taking the Holy Bible from where it sat on her bedside table. Finding the passage she wanted, she handed the book to Raskolnikov and asked him to read it to her.

Hesitantly, Raskolnikov did as she bade.

"'And so, when Jesus heard that the diseased beggar Lazarus had been put into a box, He went to stand before the cave in which the box had been stored, and He called into the dark depths of the tomb: 'Hey, Lazarus, we're going to play some ball! You like to play ball, don't you? Well, we're going to play some ball now, so if you want to play you'd better get out here

. . .' Soon the haggard figure of Lazarus appeared at the opening of the tomb, stumbling anxiously into the light of the morning sun. Shielding his eyes from the brightness, he squinted up at Jesus, eager anticipation written in his expression; clearly excited by the prospect, in a dry and rasping voice, the newly unboxed Lazarus asked, 'You're going to play some ball?' But then, shaking His head, Jesus just laughed, and as He turned to walk away, waving His hand in a gesture of casual disregard, He commented obliquely, 'We're not playing any ball . . .'"

The words sinking in, Raskolnikov blanched inwardly, sinking to the floor, feeling the bearing of his being crumpling to his core, and he thought he might vomit.

Crouching down beside him, Sonia held his head to her breast.

"You see, Rodya? Do you understand?"

"Well, well, well, what a touching picture we have here," said the figure they only just now noticed in the doorway.

"Svidrigailov!"

"The boxer and the yellow-feathered reading Bible verses," Svidrigailov said condescendingly, casually strolling into the apartment. In his arms he held a sleeping puppy, which he petted softly. "How quaint . . . I assume you've been considering my proposition, Rodya Raskolnikov?"

"Proposition?" asked Sonia.

"He knows," Raskolnikov replied. To Svidrigailov, he said, "I see you've gone with the puppy, then? So, I suppose our business proposition is moot."

Svidrigailov laughed. "I think not! But life is short, and I have decided to live large—I want your sister *and* the puppy!"

"You're mad!!"

"Hmmm . . . perhaps."

"Well, it makes no difference," said Raskolnikov, standing and helping Sonia to her feet as well, "because I'll not bow to your threats."

"But why not?!" said Svidrigailov, squeezing the puppy in frustration. "What other choice do you have!?"

Looking into Sonia's eyes, he answered, "To turn myself in. Pay for my crime, and try to make amends." Turning back to Svidrigailov, he continued, "You see, I've learned that if you're going to play ball with the Big Boys, you've got to step up and get over yourself already—or be left behind."

"Um . . . Rodya?" said Sonia. "I don't think that's what that Bible passage is supposed to mean."

"It wasn't a metaphor about baseball?"

"Well, okay, I guess near enough."

"Oh, this is very discouraging, very discouraging, indeed," growled Svidrigailov, pacing and petting his puppy far too roughly—the little dog whimpering and squirming to escape. He stopped short, a new determination in his expression. Handing the puppy to Sonia, he said, "My dear, would you look after my puppy?"

He then opened up his box, stepped boldly into it, and just as the lid was about to close completely, it swung slightly back open and he added, "His name is Feodor."

The lid slammed shut—and he was gone.

Setting the puppy on the bed, Sonia embraced Raskolnikov.

"I'm frightened," he admitted.

"I'll go with you," she said. "I will be with you—for as long as you wish me to be."

Kissing her softly on the lips, Raskolnikov slipped the again sleeping Feodor into the crook of his arm, offering the other to Sonia.

"Well, then . . . I guess we'd best get this over with."

Chapter Seventeen

Raskolnikov and Sonia arrived at the police station and were surprised to find Razumihin, as well as Raskolnikov's mother and sister, all in a frenzied state in Porfiry Petrovich's office.

"But surely he must have said something!" demanded Razumihin. "You yourself said you were the last to speak to him—last night, after we had left him!"

"Not so, not so, eh?" replied Porfiry. "For you said you then saw him on the street outside his apartment—thus, you were the last! *He-hee!*"

"Oh, yes, that's right . . ."

"But he must be somewhere!" declared Dounia. "Raz waited for him and he never came home last night."

"Oh, my poor Rodya!" cried Pulcheria, wringing her hands and dabbing her eyes with a kerchief. "Whatever has happened to my baby boy?!"

"Mother," said Raskolnikov rushing in, "it's all right—I'm here!"

"Not now, Rodya, not now!" his mother rebuked him. "This is important, and—" Realization overtook her and she ran to embrace her son, followed by all the others. "Rodya, my dear, thank heavens you're safe!"

Waving away their declarations of relief at his well-being—and the scolding for his yet again disappearing—he extracted himself from the spontaneously wrought group-hug (Porfiry Petrovich proved to be the hardest from which to free himself) and tried to get his bearings.

"But, what is all this?" he asked. "What are you doing here?"

"We thought the worst, of course," Razumihin explained, offering a friendly slap on the back. "Glad to see we were wrong again, eh, old chap? Especially after . . ." His eyes briefly glanced toward Dounia and his face colored slightly. ". . . after our discussion last night . . ."

"So then there was more that you weren't telling?" asked Porfiry.

"Yes, well, I—"

"Actually, that's what brings me here," Raskolnikov interrupted. With a deep breath—taking Sonia's hand in his for strength—he said, "Constable Petrovich . . . it was I who put the pawnbroker woman and her sister Lizaveta into the box!"

Astonished silence followed. Raskolnikov felt the sudden inclination to say he was only joking or flee, but a squeeze of Sonia's hand calmed him.

"I see . . ." commented Porfiry Petrovich, pursing his lips thoughtful-ly and appraising Raskolnikov with dire scrutiny. "I must say, this really comes as something of a surprise Rodya . . ."

"Oh, Rodya," whispered his mother, "my Rodya, how could you?"

"And how are we to know," asked Porfiry, "that this is not just another relapse of your illness? Perhaps you only *believe* you have commit-ted the crime."

"No, I'm pretty sure it was me," replied Raskolnikov. "Indeed, I can take you to where I hid the stolen loot!"

"Ah, ha! Yes, yes," said Porfiry, quite convinced. "And is there any-thing else you would like to add to your statement?"

"Well, I . . . that is . . . I really thought I would be doing a good deed—that I was making the world a better place."

"All right, good, good—and . . .?"

"Oh—um . . . and . . . I see now how I was mistaken in that, and that it was not at all my place to make such a judgment."

"Um-hmm, um-hmmm—and . . .?"

Raskolnikov could not see where Porfiry was trying to lead him until Razumihin, who had been casually shuffling closer, gave him a subtle elbow-nudge in the belly and, disguised in a mock clearing of his throat, growled, "<*Sorry!*>"

"Oh! Yes, I'm really truly sorry—and it will never happen again!"

"Huzzah! *He-hee-hee!* Good lad!" Porfiry walked over and offered a hearty handshake and a slap on the back. "Well, I think, young man, you've learned your lesson and, as you've clearly thought long and hard about the matter and punished yourself over it already, I think we can safely consider this case closed!"

"Three cheers for Raskolnikov?" suggested Razumihin—and all agreed, and so it was done.

"But one thing yet bothers me," Raskolnikov confessed. Squaring off to the police constable, he summoned his courage again and asked, "Are you . . . Porfiry Petrovich . . . God?!"

Porfiry suddenly became really quite stern, the intensity of his very bearing seeming to make him loom as a giant over them, as if the room had become dark to the brilliant sublimity of this Being before them, and he replied, "I am . . . what I am . . ."

"Blessed Savior!" cried Sonia, as she and all the others fell to their knees.

"*He-hee!*" Porfiry laughed, once again just a mere police constable. "But I'm certainly not God!"

And they all rose to their feet and shared a good laugh at the entire affair.

"So, what will you do now?" Porfiry asked.

"Well, if they're still interested," replied Raskolnikov, "Raz and Dounia and me were thinking of starting a publishing and translating enterprise."

"Of course, we're still interested!" confirmed Raz.

"But not here," Raskolnikov interjected. "Someplace where it will be appreciated more; where there isn't so much of it already and we can spread the influence of our culture and literature to new minds."

"But where then?" asked Dounia.

"Siberia!" said Raskolnikov with resolve.

"The land of opportunity!" declared Raz.

"Oh, I've always wanted to go to Siberia!" exclaimed Sonia. "Can I . . . that is . . . would you . . ."

Sweeping her into his arms, Raskolnikov gave her half a twirl (though, of course, not at all a complete 'spin', right there in the constable's office) and said, "Of course, you can come along—I'd like nothing more!"

"Ah, well—*he-hee!*" commented Porfiry with a smile. "So there's an end to it—at last!"

Raskolnikov smiled back. "Or nearly so . . ."

Epilogue

Raskolnikov slowly pushed open the door to what had been the apartment of the pawnbroker Alyona Ivanovna—surprised that it did so silently—the creak having been fixed. The interior was completely fresh and bright, a new coat of paint, new rugs on the floor, all ready for a new tenant—almost as if his crime had been completely erased, he thought, but he knew it had not . . . not expunged, merely covered over. He entered and walked to the closet where he had seen the box stashed away the last time he had visited the apartment. Would it yet be there? Only one way to find out . . .

He flung wide the door—and there it was! His heart beating wildly, for some reason his thoughts turned to Napoleon . . . and then to Lazarus . . . *(what did Sonia intend with that story after all?! Oh, well!)*

Prying at the lid, he opened it a crack and peered into the darkness. He could almost sense their presence within . . . opening it wider, light flooding in . . . Raskolnikov was disappointed to find but two skeletons and what he at first, with horror, took to be a badger! But, upon closer scrutiny, he realized it was a grotesquely obese shrew—which sneered up at Raskolnikov's interruption, then belched and rolled over and began snoring.

Closing the lid again, Raskolnikov laughed.

"Well, you have to love the irony!"

finis.

The Siberian Saga

To my beloved Marialla,

    . . . it seems so long ere I have held you in my arms . . . the winter is hard here—the cold, so vicious . . . the cold seeps down to the bones, into the soul . . . an all-consuming darkness, leaving a man bereft of e'en the hope of morning's light . . . I know not what . . . *(I thought I did once—it was a Tuesday . . . but even then—the borsht with cabbage dumplings—it was only gas . . .)* To think that now—just the mere remembrance of our summers together in our golden haven of Petersburg . . . it makes my heart ache . . . for all that is lacking in this barren wasteland—for the endless chasm in my breast, where once my heart beat only for your love . . . and the memory of you, of the perfect love we share, now echoes in the void where that heart had been . . . and, yet, my dearest darling Marialla—and, yet, it is not Siberia that makes my existence hell . . . it is my exile from splendorous you that rings and resonates through my fervid, frenzied skull—as if a big bell! *(Oh-ho-ho-ho! So very big!!)* A big bell of apoplexy, what done sprung from mine inner lacuna *de la coronary unimbrungandaniment!!. . .*

    Butanyhooo . . . I hope this letter finds you well, and, uh . . . oh—if you can, perhaps send more socks . . .

kisses,
Mish-Mish *(i.e. your little, fuzzy, snuggly-bear~)*

P.S. Father Potemkin was right, methinks . . . I really need to stop reading Bulgakov before bedtime . . .

≈

My darling Marialla,

　　. . . ah, the days here, dragging on incessantly, each indecipherable from the last—harbinger of an endless barrage of tomorrows . . . the blackened Cajun shrimp—*(excuse me)*—blackened obscurity of the Siberian night is nearly soothing to my aching soul . . . the emptiness, verily a release from the gray besmirchment of drear days—bleak, roiling waves of angst wash over as I toil at my labors in this heinous, heinous—though, truthfully, really quite savagely beautiful—no-man's land . . . But it is you, my dearest, darling dear, who sees me through—the light of your love, ever and always shining over me, in even the darkest of times . . . I can withstand hell itself, so long as I know you are out there, that you are thinking of me—missing me, as I miss you . . .

　　I must leave off now, for the work-camps start up promptly at ten—as it is, I've already missed breakfast *(but it was only their goddamned cheese omelet again—and the egg is always undercooked and runny, and I can't stomach their bloody cheese . . .)*; until next time, my love—adieu . . .

in deepest yearning,
your Mishka

My sweet Marialla,

　　. . . in this heinous, winter wasteland—the veritable waiting room to hell—you are the fire in my soul that keeps me going . . . the very thought of you warms me through—despite the endlessly falling snow . . . drifts drifting ever deeper . . . temperatures plummeting until you're just sure everything is going to shrivel up and fall off . . . And now Mosiaga *(apparently)* is getting a goiter! I'm sure he's just trying to show off for the guards—especially the new lady officer, who, surely, has risen through the ranks and is respected only because her beard comes in thicker than most of the men . . . I have informed him that the ladies don't go for what he deems "that sheik, goiter

flair!"—and I've encouraged him to paint it blue and tell others it's a Smurf
. . . *(people will still be slightly askew by it—but, rather than shrieking and
pulling out hair and running all about, the Smurf tactic generally results in
silent speculation and a slowly sauntering sort of a backing away . . .)*

But—my love!—I must now go . . . the beatings start promptly at
eight, you see, and I dare not be late—the early birds, of course, get the best
walloping . . . Write to me—write to me soon, and often! I feast upon your
words—they are my spiritual nourishment, my sole sustenance! *(aside from
the roast beef tonight—which was chewy and undercooked . . . you'd have
liked the noodles . . . the gravy was like sex in a canoe—i.e. fucking close to
water . . .)* but I digress . . .

with fondness and fondles,
your Mishka-bear

P.S. The socks were a big hit with the boys—I even managed to trade with a
guard for some vodka . . . I think if you can send underpants, I might finagle
a cigar!. . . xo~

My love, Marialla,
    . . . I have but time for a short note—as I have received your latest
letter only this moment . . . how can I resist but to reply immediately! You
say that you are mine—but no more, my darling, than I yours!. . . for you are
the heaven that awaits me, across the vast distances that separate, and the
bleak and barren eternity of winter's clutching cloy, and . . . corporeal
punishment *(perhaps)* . . . proffered in haphazard fashion *(hardly any
welts!?!)*—and the like . . . in the very summer of my soul, you are the sun,
the moon, the stars . . . you are the wind and rain, the thunder and the
lightning—you are the tempest that tempts me, bodily, mindfully, spiritually

. . . you are my Marialla . . . I, your Mishka— and when it comes to 'M&M's . . . well. . . . aren't they just the most delicious candy you can imagine! Though, you know, I would melt in your mouth—or your hand! Or any elsewhere you would have me!. . . Butanyhoo . . .

kisses and spanks *(—you're welcome!~)*,
Mishka

≈

Marialla!
 . . . O my dearest darling! I have received a letter from you today— ah, how your words resurrect me! Your love is my only nourishment! And I am a fiend—to make you suffer so . . . to just accept the decrees of fate and the dictates of my captors, leaving you there all alone . . . I weep! I weep, my Marialla! *(But, of course, a figurative—nay, a soulful—sort of weeping, due to the danger of tears freezing my eyeballs shut . . . I have seen it happen . . . and then the soldiers come, and take you for their amusement: "Vasili! Ivan! My comrades—I dare you to lick his eyeballs! Lick them and make them not frozen anymore! (Ha-ha!) I know you will not do it!" And so then they try—because they have been dared, after all, and so honor is at stake— but their tongues stick to the frozen eyeballs as if they were metal (which seems odd . . .) . . . eventually they pour vodka over the whole mess—which is very nice for the soldier and his tongue, but the poor, dumb bastard who was crying? Well, he gets it right into his eyes! And that is not so very nice. And so then they kick him in the pants or beat him in the skull, and leave him in a snow drift, and wander off in pursuit of other mischief.)*
 But I see I have lost my train of thought, my sweetheart . . . please forgive me—though I know I don't deserve it . . . *(or perhaps I do—my mind is numb, you see . . . it really is, I wouldn't lie to you about that—I'm just not the sort . . . I'm not one to shave a peach and call it a nectarine!)* I am so

very saddened to hear you feel lost without me . . . that you are bumping into things and fumbling—yet those things are not me! Oh, so long has it been ere we have had a truly fine and rugged bump and fumble! The warmth imbruing as I gaze into your milk-chocolate eyes *(which, I promise you— however tempted—I shall never lick!. . .)* . . . our bodies pressed close, flesh caressing flesh—and then lips embracing . . . the hunger of a kiss sated in the sanctity of your arms . . . writhing bodies become one in soulful synchronicity . . .

But to create such images when you are so far away is but an invitation to madness! And, anyway, I must go now, sweet Marialla . . . ere the guards return and catch me up after curfew again—once more, they said, and it's no more chocolate éclairs at morning work-break *(the heartless bastards!)* . . . but know this—because I know that you love me, I will survive this hell and one day return to you . . . and, even as I survive just knowing you love me, you, too, must be patient, taking strength, and having courage, in knowing that I love you . . . and, as such, so long as you know that I know you know I know—and conversely—our love will see us through . . .

an e'er, spiritually, a sort of cabbage bouillabaisse without you,
your beloved Mishka

P.S. It is unfortunate you were unable to send underpants—but the new shipment of socks is very lovely! Everyone says so . . . no one expected argyle, and they're a smashing success . . . Mosiaga and I are looking into the financial potential of renting them out as prostitutes!

Marialla,

    . . . I bid to you fond greetings. I have heard much about you. I was very sorry to hear the bad news regarding your goat. I wish you many fine things . . .

with sprinkles and a gumdrop,
Mosiaga

≈

Oh, my darling sweetie-pants—Marialla!!

    . . . spring has sprung, and there is a tangible magic in the air! All are affected . . . it happens every year, whene'er the temperature flirts with the freezing mark—will it aspire and transcend?. . . No, no, of course, I only jest . . . but these balmy double-digit temps certainly do bestow new life to our wearied souls! Why, just yesterday, Vasili Vladimirovich, who keeps wandering around in a daze, grumbling over this or that—something to do with a bear, I think . . . sex deprived, the bear not entirely alluring . . .? I know not what . . . but in the end, he just kills it and eats it . . . and then Mosiaga follows him about, growling like a bear! Which, of course, only infuriates Vasili Vladimirovich, and it all just spirals horribly out of control until, finally, Vasili Vladimirovich hits Mosiaga in the head with a log . . . it's terrible to have to see—especially after the third or fourth repeat—but at least it puts an end to it until consciousness returns . . . *(By the way, enclosed, my love, find a new fur coat—I hope you like it . . . I left the paws and claws intact . . . I know how eclectic your tastes run . . .)*

    Ah, and now to go out and enjoy the day! The only thing, methinks, that would be more beautiful than Siberia in the springtime—would be to have you, darling Marialla, here by my side in this savage wonderland! Perhaps—O, how I might dare to hope!—one day, when my sentence is completed, we can settle here . . . just you and I! And some chickens and a goat! *(Though such* is *how I ended up here in the first place . . .)* But, oh, still, wouldn't that be nice?. . .

your monkey-man, your slave,
Mishka

P.S. Just kidding about that living here crap—we're getting a chateau in the Crimea, dammit!

In the Land of White Death
. . . inspired by the book by Valerian Albanov

Despite the best of intentions
and the well-wishes of others,
I find myself in really rather
a drunken state after all . . .
(Not my fault, you understand—
'tis more the vodka to blame . . .)
but I feel freer and more open
to the wiles of the world
than I have since the carefree days
when I was a younger man
—or, at any rate, somewhat younger
than now I find myself . . .
(although, in the grand scheme of things,
probably still just really fucking old . . .)—
and I'd been on an expedition
heading east, north of Siberia . . .
our party had become lost,
and we were out of *hors d'oeuvres*,
the champagne nearly gone . . .
we wandered for what seemed forever;
it would have gone so much quicker
if the leader of our expedition
—his name is irrelevant . . .
mostly everyone just said: "Hey, beanhead!"—
hadn't kept stopping to write
in that damn'd journal of his . . .
(well . . . alright, then—it was me . . .);
we might have made it to Franz Josef Land
in a little over two weeks . . .

instead, by the time I eventually made it back
to Petersburg and my studies,
my mentor, Rasputin,
was just torqued beyond belief,
and as punishment he forced me
to recite the Lord's Prayer in Latin,
backwards, for three days
while having sex with unattractive,
old, hairy women with bad breath
and pustulating sores . . .

But that's neither here nor there—
for, you see, as I was saying,
I have somehow become inebriated . . .
I was out for three days last night—
and when I awoke
she was gone . . .
which somehow surprised me,
though she hadn't been there
when I'd passed out,
so I guess I just really don't know
what the hell my deal is . . .
yet, consumed by emptiness,
I have sought solace in the sacred serum
of a vial of vodka
—*(or perhaps just a bit more than that . . .)*—
and to my mind there arises
the memories of those endless nights
on the ice floes,
adrift in the godless north . . .
frigid temperatures inevitably forcing
Peter Gregorovich to snuggle closer
to Gregor Petrovich,

which caused Gregor Petrovich
to giggle and squirm—thus infuriating
the innocently warmth-seeking Peter Gregorovich,
who would then thrash at Gregor Petrovich
with his ice-hardened boot . . .
and so I faded away into slumber
to the sounds of grunts and giggles—
and when I awoke they were gone . . .
in their place, a bloated polar bear,
complacent smile upon pink-tinged muzzle,
a boot half protruding from his smirking maw . . .

But that's neither here nor there—
for I have merely run amok upon a tangent,
and, in all truthfulness,
my sole intent had been but to mention,
to both my amusement and chagrin,
I am really quite intoxicated . . .
oh, certainly, I know just what you're thinking—
"*intoxicated,*" he says, just as he was *intoxicated*
for three days last night . . .'
but I assure you, you have it all wrong—
for last night it was *she*
with whom I was intoxicated!. . .
with the gentle air of her cool composure,
and the brilliance of her beauty—
pale eyes, as the arctic sky over the open sea,
freeze me in my tracks with their intensity . . .
I can't help but to compare
the inspiration of her countenance
to the day I first sighted land
after the months of arduous travails
across snow and ice and sea—

salvation in sight,
seemingly within my eager grasp . . .
but half a verst—at most!—
separating me from all that lay in my heart . . .
yet resisting the urge to cling to my hopes
until landfall had been reached—
for as easily could it have happened
that I might drift by entirely
and be swept, once more, to sea . . .

But that's nither, hither, and *nyet*! . . .
I am nacquered, my friends—
and nacquered through and through . . .
for the wiles of a woman,
in as much as the wintry wastelands of the north,
can tear a man down—
blinding his vision
and enshrouding his thoughts
in clouded unrealities . . .
numbing him to every and all
but the familiarity of her caress . . .
squeezing his heart in her death-grip—
his life, hers to bestow or disendow . . .
his soul, to be snuffed out
upon her idlest whim . . .
and so, by need, all nacquere'd do I be—
'til in her arms I'm warmed at last
on the shores of some *southern* sea . . .

Chekhov's Pony
(a play in one act)

<u>*Dramatis Personae:*</u>

Ornre Potaninovich

Mikita Dabishavich

Irina Allinatovna

Kachka Mrakeshna

[Late summer / early autumn-ish. Nearly dusk. An estate house, high on a hill, overlooking the Sea of Azov—belonging to Ornre Potaninovich's widowed auntie (the estate house, I mean—not the Sea of Azov) . . . though she will not appear in the play, as it has overall been an intemperately cool summer, and, for the heinous knocking of her knees due to incessant shivering (no one thought to pad her knees 'til by far too late to do any good), she was all bloody, bruised, and raw, leaving crimson trails of pustulated gook in her wake where'er she slithered about, groaning and sobbing and carrying on—

But that's neither here nor there . . .
Ornre is preparing to leave at the end of the week to return home to Kiev for the winter, but there are two things he wishes to do ere he goes: witness the spectacle of Chekhov's pony, and win the hand of the beautiful Kachka Mrakeshna . . .]

[Enter ORNRE and MIKITA.]

ORNRE: "Did you know? Have you heard!? They say it will happen soon—perhaps even today!"

MIKITA: "Whatever are you going on about?!"

ORNRE: "Oh, nothing . . . I shouldn't have said—I thought you knew, is all . . . you wouldn't understand . . ."

MIKITA: *[Sternly.]* "Surely not!"

ORNRE: "But what a beautiful day—the best of the summer, I'd say!"

MIKITA: "How are your auntie's knees?"

ORNRE: "Scabbing over nicely, thank you. The doctor is saying now she may only lose the one leg . . ."

MIKITA: "Well, then—there's a bit of luck!"

ORNRE: *[Pacing impatiently.]* "Oh! Ohhh! My heart, my heart . . .!"

MIKITA: "Here, here! What, what! What's all this about your heart then? Is something wrong?"

ORNRE: "Oh, no, no—really all right…it's just that it pains me every now and again—my heart does . . . always has, really . . . it'll kill me one day, I'm sure of it . . ."

MIKITA: "Well—certainly something should! But what of your fidgeting all about? You haven't got the crabs again, have you?"

ORNRE: "Oh, no, no, I haven't, Mikita Dabishavich—something even better! I wasn't going to tell you, but I think I'll burst!" *[Whispering conspiratorially.]* "They say it's coming . . .!"

MIKITA: "That's disgusting!"

ORNRE: "No, no—I mean Chekhov's pony!"

MIKITA: "Even so . . . but tell me—is that what you're off about, lingering here by the road all afternoon? Tell me it isn't!"

ORNRE: "Oh—but it is! It is! Due to pass by at any time now . . ."

MIKITA: "Well, it's nearly sunset—if it comes any more today, it'll soon be too dark to even see the damned thing. What's so special about it, anyway?"

ORNRE: "They say it is the very pony the great Chekhov sat upon to write 'The Three Sisters'! And, anyway, even if it does come after dark, we shall at least, I think, be able to see a silhouette—and we'll certainly be able to hear it: *'clip-clop-clip-clop—braaahyee!'*"

MIKITA: "Oh! Very nicely done!"

ORNRE: "Do you think?"

MIKITA: "Well, I just said! If I'd have had my eyes closed, I almost could have smelled it, I think!"

ORNRE: "You're teasing me now . . ."

MIKITA: "No—truly, Ornre! I was about to run back to the house for my tall boots!"

ORNRE: "But I hope it shall still be light . . . do you think Irina will stop this evening? She hasn't for some time . . ."

MIKITA: "No, I—well, I'd meant to say . . . but . . . it's just that—well . . . uh!"

ORNRE: "Mikita, please! You're scaring me!"

MIKITA: "No, no—it's just . . . it's over, that's all! I've ended it, and I don't want to talk about it!"

ORNRE: "It's all right—we won't say another word . . ."

MIKITA: "She left me! Oh, I know I said it was I who ended things—but it was false bravado! I am nothing! And, besides, she used her wileful machinations to make it seem it was I—pulling away and pulling away until I couldn't stand it anymore, wondering what was going on! Did she still love me? Was she still my everything?! I didn't know—and so I would react to her pulling away, irrationally, pushing her yet further, giving her reason to put the blame on me, as if it had been I who was responsible!"

ORNRE: "She sounds devious . . ."

MIKITA: "Yes, well . . . she is, after all, a woman . . ."

ORNRE: "Uh—tush-tush! Here she comes! Ah—and with the fair Kachka!"

[Enter IRINA and KACHKA.]

MIKITA: "Irina."

IRINA: "Mikita . . . Ornre."

ORNRE: "Irina."

MIKITA: "Kachka."

KACHKA: "Mikita . . . Ornre."

ORNRE: "Kachka!! Let us go for a walk . . ."

KACHKA: "Very well—the afternoon seems to have suddenly become very chilly . . ."

[Exit ORNRE and KACHKA.]

IRINA: "How are you, Mikita Dabishavich? You're looking well . . ."

MIKITA: "Well, it seems you've moved on quickly enough—yes, I heard that you've found another lover . . . couldn't bring yourself to leave Adolph though you were 'so very deeply in love' with me, 'forever' and 'infinitely' and so many other words it is now apparent you have no idea what they mean!"

IRINA: "Who's Adolph?"

MIKITA: "But now you've just found anybody else—so long as he's not me...obviously I never meant anything to you. I was just a side-effect of your madness—an opium-inspired delusion of love, I suppose . . ."

IRINA: "You're not being fair—you know I will always be here for you, I will always be your friend . . . and I truly did love you . . ."

MIKITA: "And now?"

IRINA: "I got over it."

MIKITA: "You, with your little games, playing with the hearts and minds and souls of men! How you kept me going through the motions, jumping through your hoops each time you rang your little bell—taunting and teasing and leading me on, and long after you knew it was already over for you! You simply didn't have the integrity—or the courage—or the basic respect you claimed to hold for me—to tell me…instead pulling away—to drive me insane, pushing me to the brink, luring me into behaving foolishly, all so you could put the blame for it off on me! But I'll tell you this—I'm through with you!   I'll not be your toy anymore—I'll not be your game…you want someone else, anyone else, *everyone* else—I don't care. There's not enough left of me anymore to care . . ." *[Exits.]*

[Enter ORNRE and KACHKA.]

KACHKA: "Irina, is everything all right? Where is Mikita going?"

IRINA: "I think he has the dysentery . . ." *[Aside.]* "Which might be good, given how full of shit he is . . ."

KACHKA: "What was that?"

IRINA: "Hm? Oh, nothing—I'd better go check on him . . ."   *[Exits.]*

ORNRE: "It's almost dark now . . . and as falls the sheltering shadows of the night's soft embrace—I yet bask in the brilliance of your beauty, Kachka Mrakeshna!"

KACHKA: "Oh, my Ornrushka! You are so mellifluous in your musings!"

ORNRE: "Oh, but, my darling—it's true! Never doubt it! You are as the mystery of the night sky! The bright beacon of the stars! You are the glorious, radiant goddess of the moon—each time I am bathed in the am-biance of your beautiful brilliance, I am undone and re-made to be all you might allow!"

KACHKA: *[With a sigh.]* "Do not make me your goddess, Ornre."

ORNRE: "But—why ever not? I can think of none better . . ."

KACHKA: "To make me your goddess, it will lead you to be haunted by me—every time you look upon the light of the moon, you'll think of me—of how both it and I are unattainable, out of reach . . . and to see the dark, moonless sky, you will be reminded of what is missing . . ."

ORNRE: "But you won't be missing—you don't have to be!"

KACHKA: "I will—and I do . . . with the inevitability and constancy of the tides, I will betray you . . . such is my nature . . ."

ORNRE: "But—"

KACHKA: "You and your butts!"

ORNRE: "But nature be damned! There is nothing natural in how I love you . . . it is supernatural—*supra*-natural!"

KACHKA: "Yes . . . I suppose it really does seem that way—to you, anyhow . . . you really are something of a freak. But you'll get over me one day . . ."

ORNRE: "I won't—I will love you forever! Shall I tell you how much I love you?"

KACHKA: "Oh, please don't . . ."

ORNRE: "Even should you ever touch another, I would forgive you— simply because I love you too much to ever let foolish, human impetuosity stand in the way of such a great and glorious love!"

KACHKA: "Oh, poor Ornrushka . . ."

ORNRE: "But the man you touched? He's as good as gone—you've as much as signed his death warrant . . ."

KACHKA: "You're not being funny . . . you would never—*could* never do that!"

ORNRE: "Oh, my love, let me tell you—I'd do it in a second…but I'm not a fool—I'd make it look like an accident. But you would know, and I would know . . . and I'd make damn sure *he* would know why he was on his way out!"

KACHKA: "You're a crazy man!"

ORNRE: "I am—I am, it's true . . . crazy for you, my darling!"

KACHKA: "I don't even know who you are!"

ORNRE: "I must tell you . . . no woman I have ever loved, once she has left me, has found her 'happily ever after' . . . nothing I have done, mind you—just something, I realized, that occurs . . ."

KACHKA: "Why are you telling me this?"

ORNRE: "Because I love you! Marry me!"

KACHKA: "Well . . . yes!"

ORNRE: "Really!? Will you marry me?!"

KACHKA: "Yes! Yes!! I will marry you!"

ORNRE: "Oh! You've made me so happy! I—"

KACHKA: "No, no—I was only kidding…I was caught up in the moment, and—well, it doesn't matter. I can't marry you—honestly, I can barely stand the sight of you sometimes . . . such a lowly, loser, leprous fiend . . ."

ORNRE: "But—what are you saying?!"

KACHKA: "Well, you're not even real—here, look . . ." *[Peeling away part of ORNRE's neck.]* "You see—you're made of cardboard… not even proper cardboard, either—not even corrugated . . ."

ORNRE: "Then it's over . . . really, truly over . . ."

KACHKA: "Oh, my Ornrushka—so melodramatic . . . don't think of it as over . . ."

ORNRE: "Then, tell me, how shall I think of it?"

KACHKA: "Think as if it had never begun . . ."

ORNRE: "You know, we never even had Chinese food together . . ."

KACHKA: "I'm sorry—but perhaps it's better that way."

ORNRE: "Perhaps . . . we did have Mexican a couple of times . . ."

KACHKA: "Well, there you go!"

ORNRE: "Not really the same, though . . ."

KACHKA: "No, not really . . ."

[Enter MIKITA and IRINA.]

MIKITA: "Ornre Potaninovich! Congratulate me! Irina and I are to be wed!"

IRINA: "Ornre, are you well? You have a hole in your neck . . ."

ORNRE: "I . . . no, no—that is . . ."

KACHKA: "Oh, it's so exciting! But I thought Mikita simply had the craps? No matter—congratulations to you both! We must drink a toast to your betrothal!"

MIKITA: "The very thing! Let us go up to the house to continue the celebration with vodka and champagne! Ornre—what's the matter? You seem . . . unwell . . ."

ORNRE: "I'm just—no, I'm fine, Mikita . . . I'm happy for you both."

IRINA: "Well, whatever in the world is that?!"

[Enter a shaggy, dirty, decrepit miniature pony with tangled mane and tail, barely managing to shuffle along . . . or a dog, dressed up as a Chinese dragon . . . or a midget with horns and a cape on a pogo-stick . . .]

ORNRE: "My heart!"

MIKITA: "Is that it? Is that what you've been waiting for, Ornre?"

KACHKA: "What the hell is it?!"

ORNRE: "The pony! It's Chekhov's pony! Ahhh . . . isn't it grand . . .!"

[Exeunt.]

finis.

Anna Karenina

*. . . based on the novel by Leo Tolstoy
(along with miscellaneous influences from the likes of
Dostoyevsky and Nabakov . . .)*

Chapter One

It all began in the summer by the sea with the lieutenant's widow . . .
was a handsome woman, somewhat stern of countenance, and certainly much
more attractive by candlelight and either at a distance or right up close where
it becomes difficult to focus completely—but her form had not deteriorated
as yet and, having had numerous lovers, her experience and enthusiasm made
up for any shortcomings elsewhere. The widow's family had come from
money, so mostly Vronsky played the gigolo, paying her enough attention to
keep her paying for everything else, and went his own way the rest of the
time. It wasn't that he didn't care for the widow, for in his own unique way
he really did . . . but such was his nature: Vronsky for Vronsky's sake.

Vronsky Vronsky had grown up in Siberia—and often commented,
". . . if it can truly be said *anyone* grows up in Siberia!" and then he would
wink knowingly. But no one really ever understood what he meant by it, and
if they tried to inquire he would round on them sharply, strew obscenities
over them and, if feeling particularly bitchy, slap at them until they cried
uncle. Then he would laugh and, if they had fallen, help them back to their
feet, and pat them on the back, and brush off any dust from the floor, and call
them brother or sister or what have you, and then go on completely jovially
as if nothing had ever happened. If nothing else, he was generally great fun
at parties . . . so long as everyone remembered to keep a close eye on their
drinks and their wives—though not necessarily in that order. Vronsky could
be very Epicurean in his outlook—in that he sought out the pleasures of the
senses, believing such to be the only true path to ultimate peace of mind—yet
he lived for the moment, rarely looking to the future. He might be described

as egocentric or selfish on any number of grounds, but Vronsky was not at all an evil person. When others judged him negatively, he would always defend himself by stating that he was merely the product of society, that he was exactly what the world had made of him and, thus, should not—indeed, *could* not—be held accountable for his apparent sins; he was at best a tool of the fates, and at worst a victim of the given situation.

It was a hazy, nebulous summer—if only in the seeming of circumstance—for the weather nearly always seemed to waver between extremes. It couldn't just be hot, it had to be 110 degrees and humid, with the sun raging down over the world, baking everything in sight, and with lizards on the walls and everyone waking from siesta in the early evenings speaking in Spanish, but then panicking because they couldn't understand what they were saying (being that none of them had ever learned Spanish) . . . and it couldn't just rain, there had to be torrential showers and flooding and mudslides and tornadoes—and of course the ice storm in early August that really baffled everyone, but only lasted a couple of hours before the ungodly heat returned, so it ended up sort of okay aside from a few melted snowmen and a nasty ice-fishing incident. But Vronsky remained nearly oblivious to the oddities of his environment—indeed, he barely even noticed when the Mongol hoards invaded late in July, conquering the remote resort villa where they stayed and declaring it the capitol of their newly revived empire.

The invasion was led by a mighty warrior calling himself Chimi-khan . . . his real name, of course, was Yamyinsky Yamyangovich, and he was just a silly man with grandiose ideas—but, as no one knew of this, he was generally taken to be quite a formidable and intimidating figure. Claiming descent from Batu-khan—himself a grandson of he who had been dubbed "Manslayer" and "Master of Thrones and Crowns," the mighty "Prince of the Ocean" and the terrible "Scourge of God," that lovably ineffable man-god Chingis-khan—the uninfamous Chimi-khan swept his Mongol forces through the region, leaving in their wake a population rife with, if not terror, at least a sort of queasy uneasiness. The warrior-prince announced his intent to resurrect the Pax Mongolica—the golden age of Tatar conquest and rule—but, in truth, once his army had settled in, their actions seemed rather sluggardly. (Many began talking of the *Lax* Mongolica, and the self-professed Great Horde, heir to the centuries earlier Golden Horde, was often instead reduced to the We've-Certainly-Seen-Better-Days Horde . . .) Although the Tatars and their leader vehemently denied it, many of the natives believed them to be merely on holiday—especially given they spent the majority of their time on the beach drinking exotic, touristy drinks (the ones with little umbrellas and tropical fruit) and chasing about the local harlotry, occasionally shaking down some well-to-do passers-by for "taxes"—and hoped that perhaps they would, along with the other vacationers, leave in the autumn and return to central Asia from whence they came. But whatever their long-term plans, for the summer at least, the Mongols' authority was absolute, and Chimi-khan's word was law.

But the "Lost Mongol Invasion of the Nineteenth Century"—as it came to be known, before it was immediately and almost entirely forgotten—was really neither here nor there . . . for Vronsky Vronsky was preoccupied by other intentions—namely his own—and, all in all, was not in the clearest frame of mind. When not playing either with or upon the graces of the widow, he had found another distraction to fulfill his lustful appetites, and in spite of the way the vodka and opium tended to mute the debauchery of his fleet—though passionate and thoroughly vulgar (in as many ways as he could come up with)—tryst with the spunky and youthful Lolita, he could honestly say he found great pleasure in her company. She was a very naughty little girl, so he felt he could justify the spankings, but during his more lucid moments he wondered if, even under duress, he might ever be able to excuse the things they did with various kitchen implements; he knew she was just an innocent, hotty nymphet, so really couldn't be faulted for any wrongdoing in their endeavors, but certainly the blame could not be cast upon him either . . . or, if it could, he didn't so much care. To Vronsky, it came down to one, underlying factor: The dream we all dream, versus the life we all live. But he had decided long ago that he was going to live the dream—because, the way he saw it, if you didn't . . . well then, what the hell?!

But, once again, as with the Mongol invasion, neither the widow nor Lolita—nor the summer by the sea, if the truth be told—have much to do with anything about anything at this point . . . aside from mentioning it was upon his return to Moscow at the end of summer when Vronsky first met Anna . . .

Chapter Two

Upon the untimely death of his benefactor the widow—she seemed to have drowned . . . and little wonder, as it no doubt proved impossible to swim after she had been mysteriously impaled by an oar . . . (*Chimi-khan professed complete ignorance and innocence with regard to the mishap, though he was ever after being accused of not having both oars in the water . . .)*—Vronsky had packed up a few of her belongings and headed back to the city. He knew it would be a harsh and tearful farewell that he must bid to lovely Lolita; he would never forget her and certainly she would find it forever impossible to get over her love for him, but, even so, he decided to go easy on himself and just slip away in the night. It was on the train to Moscow, as he sat in silent lament, feeling regret—in his loins, if not his heart—over having failed to say goodbye to his most recent love, that he met Oblonsky . . . and it was Oblonsky, in turn, who introduced Vronsky to his sister Anna when they had reached the Moscow station . . .

"Anna!" Oblonsky hollered into the crowd as he and Vronsky stepped from the train with their bags. At first Vronsky was unable to determine whom, exactly, the man who had shared his compartment on the train was calling to. In a moment, a woman stepped forward through the bustling throng, and Oblonsky quickly moved toward her. He seemed about to hug her, but caught himself in time from embarrassing them with such a public display of affection—such was not at all deemed proper, and instead he merely took the hand she proffered and leaned in to bestow a light peck on her cheek. "Anna! It's so good to see you, and wonderful that you've come to greet my return . . ."

Vronsky was completely aware as Oblonsky rambled on excitedly, but he could not have repeated after what had been spoken. From the moment Anna stepped free from the crowd, he felt mesmerized, held captive in the essence of her poise and beauty. All the women he had ever known immediately became absent from his mind—for put next to any other, Anna was a divine princess in a world of leprous hags whose aspects could do little but scathe at his desire. His entire being seemed filled with her, and the rest of the world ceased to exist. He drank her in and became instantly intoxicated—by her porcelain smooth flesh, her slender waist and full bosom, her piquant lips—like succulent cherries—her luxuriant hair flowing like liquid chocolate . . . she was his sole sustenance.

And then her eyes met his, and in so doing she returned his soul to him; at first they seemed flat and dull, but when they connected with Vronsky's own eyes there was a spark of luminosity, and, with life restored, they glowed brilliantly. Vronsky's heart beat madly, and when she lowered her eyes, her cheeks flushing a guilty shade of pink, he knew she had sensed the passion he felt for her.

Reality returned abruptly to the fingers of Oblonsky snapping annoyingly in Vronsky's face, and he realized the man had been trying to get his attention for some time—though he seemed oblivious to the reason behind Vronsky's distraction.

"Ah, good, there you are! I thought for sure we'd lost you," Oblonsky said, smirking, as Vronsky tore his attention from Anna. "Did you hear? Were you even paying attention to what Anna was saying about the poor unfortunate who fell onto the tracks, right under our train?" He frowned, but with the hint of his smirk returning. "Are you sure you're all right? You seem somehow off in your own little world . . ." Oblonsky seemed overly proud to have noted Vronsky's dreamy abstraction—and amused to have called him on it.

"Yes, yes, I'm fine," Vronsky replied, waving away Oblonsky's taunting. "I was merely thinking how rude it was of you to neglect to introduce me to this lovely woman before us, and I'm afraid I got rather caught up in it . . ."

"Hmf!" Oblonsky snorted in embarrassment. "Yes, well, I was just getting to that." Recovering his composure, he continued, "Anna, dear, I would like you to meet my *erstwhile* traveling companion Vronsky Vronsky; Vronsky, my sister Anna." Vronsky could tell Oblonsky felt very superior to have conducted the introduction in the manner he had, but there had been too much emphasis on the word "erstwhile"—which is a silly word anyway, and should rarely (if ever) be used—as if to say that Vronsky could not become a part of the past tense soon enough . . . but Anna was extending her hand toward him, offering the hint of a curtsy, and the brother was struck from his thoughts.

"It's a pleasure to meet you, Mr. Vronsky," Anna said, her voice soft and warm like honey, verily melting him where he stood.

Taking her delicate fingers in his hand, their touch sending a thrill of electricity through him, he bowed gracefully, raising her hand to his lips and softly kissing it. Feeling the shiver that coursed through her as he did so, he smiled and replied, "And my pleasure in making your acquaintance wells up within from the very bowels of my being, creating a moistness in my pants, as if of bold endeavors and crude intentions . . ."

"Oh, dear!" Anna exclaimed, aghast, her eyes widening and color rising in her cheeks—though she did not withdraw her hand until Vronsky began licking it. "I . . . I don't think I understand . . ."

"That's fine, Anna," Oblonsky grumbled, moving with deliberateness to stand between Vronsky and his sister. He acted as if he felt he should be enraged by Vronsky's audacity, but instead gave in to the confusion of his surprise at the turn of events. "I believe what Mr. Vronsky meant to say was that the pleasure is all his."

"Oh, on the contrary," Vronsky corrected him, peering over Oblonsky's shoulder and leering at Anna; "I'm extremely willing to share my pleasure . . ."

This second affront to Anna's honor put Oblonsky over the edge. His anger leaving him flustered, he began sputtering nearly unintelligible rantings regarding the sanctity of marriage and, thus, the propriety of not indulging in perverse innuendoes toward married persons, and he ushered his sister quickly away from so base a character.

Bogged down by his luggage, Vronsky could not maneuver through the crowds at the station as well, and he soon lost sight of the object of his affectation—but not before he saw Anna turn around to glance back at him, a look of disappointment or regret in her eyes. Discouraged by his failed pursuit, Vronsky sat thoughtfully on a nearby bench, wondering how next to proceed. His fingers absently stroking his bearded chin, Vronsky mused aloud, "Now, what did that Oblonsky fellow say her husband's name was . . .?"

Chapter Three

Vronsky Vronsky was not, in actuality, without a certain moral integrity; he held his own code of conduct, and felt the rules governing society didn't apply to himself. It could be said his greatest sin was that of pride, for he saw himself as more than the common rabble—his spiritual essence burned with a brighter intensity than that of others, and thus he was in a position to judge the actions and motives of his fellow man. Beyond that, he merely treated others in the manner he decided they deserved to be treated. The widow had used him as much as he had used her, and Lolita had been mature beyond her thirteen years, so, he believed, she was fully able to make her own decisions—surely the wisdom of experience more than compensated for any drawbacks arising from a premature lessening of innocence. Vronsky could rationalize every act he performed and every thought that passed through his mind to make the situation seem to shine in his favor— though he rarely bothered to do so consciously; it was a sort of intuitive sense he possessed allowing him to always be aware of the balance of justice within those around him. Because Vronsky had been blessed by the fates to hold such a wondrous power—as he saw it—he would never allow himself to become romantically involved with another man's wife . . . unless, of course, the other man was undeserving of her. If the husband cheated on his wife, or failed to love and respect her and hold her in the proper esteem, Vronsky judged him to be unworthy . . . and if sparks should fly between Vronsky and the wife—well, he could never understand how it might be considered adultery if the marriage was a sham in the first place.

The moment Anna's eyes had lit up when she had been introduced to him, Vronsky was sure her marriage fell into such a category—and, thus, she was free to love another. He felt determined to see that that other would be him . . . And so it was that Vronsky found his way to the offices of Anna's husband, Karenin, merely to confirm his beliefs with regard to the man . . .

"So you're a friend of Oblonsky's," Karenin said—for such was how Vronsky had introduced himself. With a tight grimace that might have been an attempt at a smile, Karenin motioned for Vronsky to sit, and added, "It's been a while—how did you last leave him?"

"I saw him as recently as yesterday," Vronsky replied, accepting the cigar Karenin proffered him. "He seemed slightly vexed on some point—though having just returned to the city, I suppose it is to be expected."

"Ah, yes," Karenin said, frowning. "I heard about that nasty business at the railway station yesterday—the poor man who was killed."

"But, of course, you would have heard—your wife was there to meet Oblonsky..."

"Hmm? My wife?" Karenin seemed confused. "Oh, well, I'm sure she was—it sounds like something she would do, anyway . . . actually I read about the incident in the morning paper."

"Yes, surely it would have also been there." Vronsky smiled, beginning to feel ever more confident his impressions had been true. "I had the pleasure of making your wife's acquaintance as well; she seems a remarkable woman . . . really very extraordinary . . . quite nubile . . ."

"What?!" Karenin's attention had lapsed momentarily, but Vronsky had now regained it. "What do you mean?"

"Oh, nothing, naturally," Vronsky replied, waving away the man's gruffness. "Oblonsky just raved about her the whole time on the train."

"Ah . . ." There was a moment of awkward silence, while Karenin seemed to be trying to think of something else to say. Finally, he began standing up again and said, "Well, thank you then, for stopping by. If you should see Oblonsky, be sure to give him my regar—"

"Oh, but wait," Vronsky said quickly. "I've come for a reason. You see, your brother-in-law was kind enough to recommend you to me when he heard I was looking for employment. I'm between positions just now, you see, and he said surely a man with connections as yours would have no difficulty in placing me somewhere."

"So you're looking for a job, are you?" Karenin asked, sitting back down and scratching his head thoughtfully. "What sort of work are you thinking of?"

"Well, I'm not exactly sure—that is, I have an idea of what I'd like to be doing, but I'm not at all sure what it's called." Vronsky slumped down in his chair and stared off into space, as if trying to recall the job title of his would-be profession, all the whole while puffing on his cigar and blowing little smoke rings. "You'll know what it is, I'm sure," he continued. "Like one of those jobs where you sit at a desk, and you shuffle about a lot of papers and jot down a bunch of figures . . ."

"A . . . a bookkeeper?" Karenin ventured.

"Well, yes, but . . . no. Not exactly a bookkeeper. The job where you might occasionally have to write some kind of report about something or other, but it really has no bearing on anything or anyone anywhere, which is fine because it's all so full of rambling and babbling double-talk it doesn't make any sense anyway . . ."

"Oh!" Karenin declared, brightening. "You're talking about a government clerk!"

"Yes! That's it—a government clerk! I'd like to be that for you, if I could."

"Well, I don't know that I really have the authority to be hiring government clerks," Karenin replied, scrunching up his face in thought, "what with me being a private businessman and not a government official. Tell me, have you ever served in the military?"

"Oh, of course," said Vronsky. "I was in the navy for a time; I was stationed in the Pacific." It was a lie, but he had gotten into a fight over a prostitute with a sailor in Guam several years earlier, and in his mind it seemed close enough not to split hairs.

"Good, good," Karenin said, nodding his head. "That's sure to help things along. I'll tell you what I'll do—I have some friends . . . in particular, a certain general who might be able to pull some strings."

"I am deeply indebted to you, Karenin," said Vronsky, standing and offering his hand. "You're everything I knew you would be."

"Well . . . pish-posh!" Karenin waved away the seeming compliment, again acting gruff but obviously pleased. "Why don't you come by the house tomorrow evening—my secretary can give you the address—and I'm sure I will have heard something by then. Say about six? You'll stay for dinner, of course?"

Vronsky smiled. "I'd be delighted . . ."

Chapter Four

Everything was shaping up exactly as Vronsky had hoped. After winning his way into the center of Anna's societal life—through an unwilling Oblonsky and an unwitting Karenin—Vronsky found himself in the flexible and extremely opportunistic position of *friend of the family*; from such a standpoint he could very easily find all sorts of seemingly casual and unadulterous reasons to just pop in whenever he would like and, as long as he was there, steal a few hours of Anna's time. The fact he had taken an apartment within mere blocks of the Karenins and now held a prestigious— and undemanding—government post only served to make the situation all the easier. . .

The afternoons he spent with his Anna—for such was how he now thought of her . . . not as the wife of another man, but as his very own, the love of his life, for whom he had waited so long—filled Vronsky with unsurpassable joy. Just getting to know her, talking to her, looking into her beautiful eyes . . . and if she should forget herself for a moment in the girlishly giddy excitement of telling a story and lay her soft hand upon his arm—well, such would overcome Vronsky's emotions to such a degree he would immediately vow to himself never again to visit the prostitute Sonia— with whom he had struck up a relationship to tide him over until he had completely won Anna's heart, thus allowing things to really heat up between them. On one occasion, when she had spilled a few drops of tea on Vronsky's hand as she handed him the cup, Anna had then proceeded to lap up the drops with her tongue—after which she laughed, embarrassed, and told him they were now even, as he had licked her at their first meeting. It was that day, Vronsky knew, she was getting near to taking him as her lover, and so delighted was he that he lasted six whole days—rather than the usual two—before he broke down, forgot about the vow he'd made, and returned to his whore.

As much as he loved Anna, and as much as he yearned to spend every possible moment with her, it was her society parties he truly hated— and yet the longing in his heart urged him to tolerate them as best he could.

"Well, then," said Oblonsky as they retired after dinner to the sitting room, "how about a riddle?" Oblonsky was one of Anna's half a dozen or so guests that evening; he was joined by Kitty, who was Oblonsky's sister-in-law, and Levin, Kitty's betrothed. And, of course, there was Vronsky—who was grateful that Karenin, as usual, was absent. There were also three or four others whom Vronsky did not know; he had been introduced, but they were inconsequential and generally stayed at the periphery of the group, not so much ever getting directly involved as merely mumbling incoherently in approval or negation over the current subject of conversation. Much to Vronsky's chagrin, all seemed quite taken with Oblonsky's idea.

"Oh, do! Do!" squealed Kitty, bouncing up and down, clapping her hands. Vronsky was greatly intrigued by Kitty—at eighteen she was near enough to a nymphet, all perky and ripe and inspiring of so many naughty thoughts, that he could not help but smile at her youthful exuberance. She was, however, a source of no small amount of vexation to him, as he found her breasts to be so very, very enticing they caused him to doubt his love for Anna. "I love riddles!" she added, gaily.

Anna smiled—though whether in actual approval because she, too, loved riddles, or out of polite patience to cover the annoyance of Kitty's juvenile, superficial simplicity, Vronsky didn't know—and replied, "All right, let's."

"Okay, I'll begin," Oblonsky said, rubbing his hands together, with a gleam in his eyes that, in anyone else, might be mistaken as cleverness. "So, you're running through the forest; you're completely naked—"

"Oh, enough already!" Vronsky shouted, leaping from his chair and startling everyone. "My god! Politics and gossip and gossip about politics and the politics of gossip . . . and now we have to suffer through *riddles* as well? Well, then, Oblonsky—here's the answer to your mind-bending dilemma: You piss on the badger! And while you're at it . . . piss on your riddle—and piss on you! How does anyone in Moscow ever manage to stay sane with such utterly futile drollery always pinning one down?! It's enough to make a man want to scream and cry and vomit and thrash his fists on his face and bludgeon his neighbor and tear at his clothes and curse at the clergy and spit on the Holy Patriarch's divine grace! For the love of god—enough, I say!!"

The outburst was, at first, met by utter silence. But after a moment Oblonsky, his feathers rumpled like a dirty, humbled grouse in disarray, grumbled, "Oh, Well . . . I . . . that is . . ."

"And well said, my friend," said Vronsky, slapping him on the back. "Always thinking, aren't you . . . you quick-witted, oblong, old bastard, you . . ."

Kitty sprang to her feet and before he knew it Vronsky was confronted by a lovely but stern finger being waggled scoldingly in his face. "Mr. Vronsky, you're behaving absolutely abominably!" she spat at him; too young to be aghast like the rest, she settled into an irascible irritability. "If you don't care for the conventions of society, perhaps you'd care to enlighten us as to how you backwater *Siberians* pass your evenings?"

Although aroused by her temerity—not to mention the way she angrily pursed her tantalizing lips—Vronsky frowned, casting a dour glance over her that seemed to say, *"You impertinent, little tart, you are as less than nothing to me, and I don't know why I even tolerate you (other than because of your breasts, of course), but perhaps I might yet find some amusement in you, so let's just see where this goes then . . ."* But what he said was: "Mostly we fight for our daily survival . . . in our spare time, if we have any energy left from the travails of the day, we wrestle with bears—unless we're lucky enough to stumble across a yeti—and we eat tacos and drink vodka, and we fuck."

Kitty's mouth dropped open and her eyes nearly bulged from their sockets to be spoken to in such a manner. The entire room sat in stunned silence.

Laying a hand gently on Vronsky's arm, Anna softly began, "Vronsky, I don't think—"

"I'm sorry, Anna," Levin interrupted, getting to his feet. His face was flushed by restrained lividity. "But I'll not stand by and listen to this obnoxious so-and-so speak to a lady that way—not to any lady, of course, but I'll certainly not put up with it directed at my Kitty!"

"Ah, ha! At last—the country gentleman," Vronsky said, an expression of relief replacing one of belligerent exasperation. "And how right you are—I've been a fool . . . a loud-mouthed, sweaty, under-deodorized and nearly flatulent fool. Absolutely priggish. And I apologize to all of you— even you, Oblonsky, you great, chunky bear, you—but most of all to Kitty . . ." Turning to her and taking her hands in his, he knelt before her with utter humility and remorse, tears streaming down his cheeks. "Kitty, dear Kitty, I've been horrible and I really, truly am so very sorry; I know I'm completely reprehensible—but do you think there is any possibility at all you might perhaps find it in the purity of your beautifully immaculate heart to forgive me?"

Blushing to suddenly find herself the center of attention, the remainder of the evening dependant on her answer now, with a tearful man on his knees before her, Kitty could barely find the words to reply. She seemed to want to remain angry with him, but to see how intently he stared at her breasts, she crumbled—how could she doubt his sincerity? . . . "Well, I . . . I mean . . ." she stammered, "I suppose I—"

"Oh, thank you!" Vronsky cried, grasping her close and burying his face in her belly. "You are my savior!" he declared, climbing to his feet and bestowing the lightest, most tender of kisses on her forehead. "Well, then," he said, with a sigh, taking his place once again beside Anna. "Now that that's over with . . . let's get back to the rest of this riddle of yours, Oblonsky; does anyone remember where we'd left off?"

Everyone thought about it for half a moment—still slightly at a loss by the whole display that had just unraveled before them—and finally Anna replied, "I think we . . . we were completely naked . . . weren't we?"

"Ah—indeed, indeed!" Vronsky agreed excitedly, beginning to unbutton his shirt. "Now *this* is my kind of party! . . ."

Chapter Five

With regard to the duality of existence—specifically the contrary views of, on the one hand, a belief that all things have significance of some sort, that all events are for some purpose, that basically everything has some level of importance toward a distinct or predetermined end, versus, on the other hand, the idea that we're all just schlepping along, that life is entirely and completely random: The latter view of course obliterates the former, though the two are in complete contradiction—or rather because they are in contradiction—just as chaos always, by its very nature, must destroy order; yet, even so, it is important to note even as such as it is, the former also simultaneously inhibits or binds the latter, which is the innate design (or intent) of order, to confine chaos. Thus it can be stated, each acts in antithesis to the other, creating a sort of paradox of being and such, therefore, is how we exist—as "Prisoners to the Paradox of Being."

This concept of the duplicity of being—or the yin and the yang of it as it were—does not, however, arise from any sort of inherent, universal Truth governing existence. Instead, it originates from the opposing forces of the infinite plenitude of spirituality and the finite needs and wants of physicality. The spiritual state, unhindered by the limitations of physicality, constitutes a state of being that is Everything; no judgment of right or wrong-doing can be applied, because there is not the same impetus toward competition and selfishness that arises with corporeal existence. It is only when the spiritual takes physical form in the universe—and becomes ruled by the strictures of science and vulnerable to the necessities and desires of physicality—that the inner soul strives to break free of its boundaries and re-attain some of its lost power of infinity. Thus, although it seems opposite of that which one might first suppose, order arises from the unencumbered essence of the supernatural state, or spirituality, and chaos arises from the restrictions imposed by the natural state, or physicality.

To exist in a universe in which the metaphysics of its very make-up lie in contradiction ensures such a complex infrastructure of being—due to the interwoven intricacies of the ontological and the cosmological factors involved—that the probability of any sort of integral atrophy is practically impossible. And to discover himself living in a world that exists in such a universe, where the coexistence and codependence of the spiritual and physical operate in a union of perfect balance, Vronsky Vronsky found his own being to be really rather epistemologically precarious. In his own mind, by some innate sense of existential necessity, Vronsky believed he must remain slightly removed from reality; to become directly embroiled within the intricate mechanism that is human existence would be to skew his perceptions, disallowing the moral imperative he possessed over others. Even so, no matter how vehemently he might try to escape it, the essence of physical being inevitably permeated to some degree any sort of superficiality that arose as a result of internal illusions and misrepresentations cast over him by the disrupting influence of his own inner spiritually; to take an active role as a participant in life—as opposed to merely acting as an observer, which in and of itself can even offer too great a residual influence—would often leave Vronsky unknowing, and therefore unconvincing, in said role . . .

And, so, instead, despite the pull of his inner self, which created a yearning within to be more than merely human, Vronsky surrendered himself to the desires of his finite, corporeal being and just hoped for the best . . . though in the darkest recesses of his troubled psyche, he always feared that somehow, in some way, if he should miss-step and stray too far from the path of his enlightenment, dire consequences would be in store . . .

Chapter Six

Vronsky's obsession—which he of course took for love—grew at a startling rate, his heart swelling, nearly exploding, with emotion at the very thought of Anna. By day, he schemed and calculated how to make her his own, and by night she filled his dreams . . .

He dreamt of her, as usual, one night about a week after she had first surrendered herself to him completely . . . only it wasn't exactly Anna—it was what he wished she could be; it was someone new, yet in that subtle way dreams have, she was cast in familiarity. She nuzzled close, and he felt his buttocks being squoze in the loving grasp of her fingers, even as he heard her approving purr. Her lips brushed softly over his and he felt the sweet warmth of her breath. A spark of electricity arced from her dazzling eyes, igniting the fires of passion within him. Darkness closed in all around as he took her rigorously into his embrace. Shutting his eyes, he felt overcome by the glorious scent of her perfume. The heat of her longing burned through him, making his body tingle, his mind reel. Floating in a stasis of growing urgency, they held one another for a momentary eternity, lost in a mutual outpouring of kinetic desire . . . but the gods were angry and would not allow this love to continue, sending forth Momus—the god of mockery, that ignoble, hair-flipping, little bag of shit—to work his mischievous magic over them. Suddenly there were monkeys everywhere—and not regular monkeys either . . . these were really scary monkeys, with goat horns and snake tongues and scorpion tails and lobster claws for hands and vulture talons for feet. Although not of unusually large size—each ranging from two to three foot tall—they possessed tremendous strength and amazing speed and agility and they did not, as normal monkeys might, chirp and hoot and screech, but instead growled and roared like the most savage of bears. A ghastly green glow emanated from the evil monkey minions of Momus, making them appear as grim specters from the very bowels of the netherworld and their eyes—large, black pools of emptiness—held Vronsky's soul in the clutches of their chilling grip. They swarmed around the two lovers in a melee of chaos and ill intent and the fear coursed through him, rising like bile in his gorge and tasting like a particularly sulfurous egg drop soup. And then the demonically mutated lower primates were upon them, attacking with a staggering vehemence that made Vronsky's and Anna's flesh burn with infernal pain.

And then they were walking on the beach, her hand held comfortably in his own, and there were no nasty, evil, little monkeys anywhere in sight, but only sun and surf and sand and the two of them. Except now she was no longer Anna—nor even the not exactly Anna she had been—but instead seemed to be Vronsky's cousin Evdokia . . . which was all right with Vronsky, as it was only a dream and, quite frankly, he had always wanted Evdokia anyway (but strictly in the carnal sense of wanting someone), ever since they had played 'doctor' that summer down by the Sea of Okhotsk when they were yet horny, experimenting adolescents—as opposed to now when he was a horny, experienced adult. They were naked—but in that casual sort of dream-naked in which neither of them had the impression the other's erogenous zones were staring at them—and so they had sex in nine different languages. He lost himself completely in the oasis of her love, his entire universe centered around the bright sunlight glistening off her tanned flesh, moist with perspiration, and the glow of insatiable excitement in her eyes, and the gritty, sandy dryness of her hair (that really needed to be washed after romping around on the beach as they had been). She began speaking to him in Latin—but he had never studied that language, so it was all Greek to him; Momus, however, was not to be denied, and at the god's psychic urging Vronsky and Evdokia both suddenly remembered they shared a common set of grandparents. Thoroughly disgusted by the sinful atrocity they had engaged in, they made love one last time and ran screaming down the beach in opposite directions . . .

Time passed . . .

. . . Vronsky stopped screaming and slowed to a walk. Instead of the beach, he found himself wandering through a giant maze. Making his way to the center, he was confronted by a gigantic ladybug who wore the face of Lizaveta Proknokovnia—his shrewish, consumptive landlady—and she was singing bawdy, burlesque songs about little girls and ponies and premature death and incest and adultery and the like... he knew for sure she intended to eat him, but just then, from out of nowhere, he was surrounded by a pack of wild prostitutes—though not your regular, everyday, run-of-the-mill prosti-tutes . . . instead they were really scary prostitutes, with goat horns and snake tongues and scorpion tails and lobster claws for hands and vulture talons for feet; they possessed tremendous strength and amazing speed and agility, and they did not, as normal prostitutes might, gasp and moan and scream, but instead growled and roared like the most savage of bears . . .

And then Vronsky again abruptly found himself on the beach, only the beach was a maze, and Anna was with him—except she was a giant, singing ladybug with two heads—one which held really a very close likeness to her, and the other that seemed more a version of all she might be if she could be more than she was—and she ate him. It was in her stomach that the Doctor told him he had gout—and, of course, Vronsky believed him (though if he had stopped to think about it, he would have realized just how outra-geous a claim it really was . . .), for he had known the Doctor ever since they had played "evdokia" that summer down by the Sea of Okhotsk when they were yet horny, experimenting interns . . .

It was then that Vronsky's goiter popped and he slipped in the pus, falling down and hitting his head. The pain was horrendous—but in a dream-pain kind of way . . . so really just rather frustrating and incessant and bothersome; on the brighter side, it seemed to make him omnipotent! Vronsky stood to discover the doctor had become Manuel—whom he didn't know—and he was wearing a dress and a wig, and it just gave Vronsky such a case of the chilly-willies that he shook himself right awake.

It was just before dawn and Vronsky felt exhausted, flustered, and, as usual, aroused. He was to meet Anna that morning in the park and decided he should take a walk to clear his mind and allow the lingering uneasiness of his nightmare to dispel. As he dressed he failed to notice in the dark gloom of his apartment the other man lying in his bed . . .

Chapter Seven

Vronsky Vronsky Vronsky Vronsky watched silently as his source, his primary self—the being from which the doppelganger had assumed his identity—put his clothes on and left. He smiled. The time to act was close at hand—but for now, for a little while longer, he would have to hold his patience. There were yet plans to be made and refined . . . he would have to continue to observe his prey and those associated with him, though it would be more difficult now, on his own as he was . . . far easier he felt to watch from the safety of within. But this would be better, he thought . . . free to move about . . . free to take action . . . when the moment was right . . .

Without a moment to lose, the Second Vronsky dressed quickly and followed the First Vronsky. The First was already well out of sight before the doppelganger managed to get out to the street, but it didn't matter—up until only a few short hours ago, when he began separating himself from his host, he shared all the same memories, and thus he knew the destination toward which Vronsky—the original—now headed.

The Second Vronsky reached the park and circled the long way around to get to the location of the appointed rendezvous so as to approach undetected. This taking quite some time, when he arrived, sneaking up silently and hiding in the nearby bushes, the First Vronsky and Anna were already deeply involved in conversation . . .

"Then . . . you don't love me!" Vronsky accused, clutching Anna's hands in his own, but turning away as if thoroughly distraught. "It's all right, you can tell me . . ."

"Oh, no, no, Vronsky, my dear!" Anna pleaded, pulling him to her. "You know I have never loved a man as I love you!"

"Ah, yes," Vronsky beamed. "The blindfold and the shackles . . . you'd mentioned you enjoyed them . . ."

"That was nice, yes—nice, yet very naughty . . ." Her eyes gleamed at the remembrance, but her face flushed a guilty crimson. "But I speak now of my heart and my soul, and not merely my body!"

"All in all, it wraps up into a nice little package . . ." Vronsky noted, eyeing her up and down.

"Oh! You're insatiable!" Anna scolded. "You're such a beast sometimes, Vronsky!"

"*Grrrrr!*" he agreed, biting at her neck.

"Stop it!" she cried, pushing him back. "What if someone sees?!"

"To hell with someone!" Vronsky announced vehemently. "Whoever he is! And to all the someones—and to all their friends, as well! I love you—that's all that should matter. . . and if a man can't even bite the neck of the woman he loves—well, then, I just don't know what!"

"But what about my husband?"

"I was never all that fond of him, actually . . . he'll have to bite his own neck . . ."

"You know what I mean," she said, feigning exasperation, yet unable to completely hide her smile. "I don't think I could ever leave him—not because I love him, but a divorce would make me an outcast from society . . . and I don't think I could stand that. I'm just so confused; being with you feels so right, when you kiss me and touch me and make love to me . . . but at the same time, it seems so and dirty and . . . oh, I just don't know what I should do!"

"Oh!" Vronsky declared, amused. "My silly, little duck! That's how it's supposed to feel—it's an *affair* . . . it feels so good because it's just so *baaad!*"

"Just make your fun then!" Anna cried, surging to her feet and confronting him sternly. "You don't care at all what I might be going through! The pressure I have to suffer to make sure we don't get caught! So long as you get what you're after, you don't care what happens to me!"

She started to storm away, but Vronsky intercepted her. "No, Anna, that isn't true at all," he soothed her, taking her into his arms and kissing away her tears. "You know you're the world to me. I only make light of the matter to try to lift your spirits." Guiding her back to the bench, he asked, "Have you given any more thought to what we talked about the other day? About going to Italy for a month? Perhaps a holiday will help you sort out your feelings . . ."

"I don't know, my love," Anna sighed, leaning her head on his shoulder. "Do you really think we could sneak off together like that? And would it even do any good?"

"Of course, it would do you wondrous good to get away for a while—it would do *us* wondrous good; I believe a great deal of the angst you feel over our relationship is that it's fallen right smack dab into the middle of your old life . . . we need some time to ourselves to create a fresh setting for our love. And, as for getting away, all you'd have to do is tell your husband you want to travel in Italy for a few weeks, for the climate or the culture or— well, it doesn't really matter . . . he barely notices you when you're here, why should he be bothered to find you gone?"

"Vronsky, that's a horrible thing to say!"

"Yes, but is it true?"

"Hmmm . . . yes, I suppose it is . . ."

"And I'll start a carefully placed rumor to lead people to the conclusion I'm in Petersburg on business or something." Kissing her forehead, he added, "We'll make it all work out . . . you'll see."

"All right, then—you've convinced me!" Anna declared. "We'll go to Italy! Oh, I'm so excited!" Offering a quick kiss before snuggling her head back into the sheltering nook of his shoulder, she asked, "Oh, Vronsky, my love . . . what did I ever do to deserve you?"

Having heard enough, the Second Vronsky quietly crept back out of the bushes. Everything was going according to plan . . . not that he really had a plan exactly, but if he had things certainly seemed to be shaping up in such a manner as to be pointing in a direction seemingly conducive to what he would have probably been generally thinking . . . or so he hoped. In any event, his nemesis, his second self—or rather he corrected himself grudgingly, to be entirely accurate, his *first* self, as he, in truth, was the actual second—would soon be out of the picture for a time, providing ample opportunity for Vronsky Vronsky Vronsky Vronsky to carry out his nefarious schemes . . . although, he realized, first he would have to come up with some idea as to what those nefarious schemes might be—but there would be time for that as well. First things first, his thoughts were jumbled and confused—he needed nourishment . . . something sugary and sweet perhaps, for energy. And then he knew he would be needing some money—which should be easy enough to come by . . . possibly he could find something back at the apartment to pawn . . . a chair or some spoons or—the axe the landlady kept by the front door . . . that, surely, would fetch a goodly price . . .

"What did you do to deserve me, my dear Anna?" the doppelganger mused, as he strolled happily from the park. "God's angry—He sent me! . . ."

Chapter Eight

Whereas Vronsky Vronsky was not, at heart, a religious sort of man—his personal philosophy stemming more from an instinctual impetus that nearly entirely precluded any need to consciously rationalize his behavior—Vronsky Vronsky Vronsky Vronsky, on the other hand, was actually an extremely devout individual. Having risen from the very primordial essence of the First Vronsky's soul—like a sticky sort of something one might find clinging to the bottom of his shoe—the demon swore his fealty to the spirit of a long-dead god who had been past his prime already when humans first joined together in the earliest cities and civilizations. He had been an angry, fearful sort of god, and though over the centuries (and with death . . .) he had mellowed somewhat, he could still be quite a nasty bastard at times; of his vassal on Earth, the same might be said. Thus it was on the day following the departure of the First Vronsky and his lover Anna on their romantic holiday abroad that the Second Vronsky sought to usurp the position of his primary self in Muscovite society . . .

"Ah, Vronsky," Oblonsky declared, running up to the doppelganger and grabbing at his arm as if to make certain he was real. "You're still here! Good, good . . . I had feared I might miss you."

"Well, Obbie!" the Second Vronsky replied, batting his eyelashes and placing his hand on Oblonsky's own, which still clutched his arm. "I never realized before how you truly felt . . ."

Oblonsky quickly withdrew himself several paces, brushing at non-existent lint on his suit and shuffling his feet. "I mean . . . well, that is . . . oh, bother! You know that isn't what I meant! I had heard you were to leave for Petersburg yesterday, that you would be gone for the entire month."

"My plans were delayed," the Second Vronsky explained. "Indefinitely."

"Well, it's delightful to know you'll yet be with us," Oblonsky said, seeming relieved somehow—probably, the doppelganger realized, because he had figured the Petersburg story to be a hoax, and that Vronsky would be with his sister . . . and if an obtuse bean-head like Oblonsky could see through the charade, surely anyone could. Of course, it really didn't matter anymore, as the Second Vronsky had taken the First's place, and by the time the First returned, the Second planned to have some way of more permanently ridding himself of his double . . .

"I don't believe you know my associate," Oblonsky continued, indicating the young man with him. "This is Alyosha, a student at the seminary, who is helping out with some clerical tasks at my office. Alyosha, this is Vronsky."

"It's a pleasure to meet you, Mr. Vronsky," said the young man politely, offering his hand.

"Well!" Vronsky declared, almost laughing as he accepted Alyosha's hand to shake. "You seem rather the monkly little fellow, don't you! But please, call me Vronsky."

At the doppelganger's touch, Alyosha shivered, feeling an icy knot tie itself into his intestines. His smile gave way briefly to an unsettled frown before his face drained entirely of color, puckering into an expression of intense consternation. Taking back his hand, he used it to hold in the contents of his bowels as he loped off mumbling an incoherent apology.

"What a queer little monkey," the Second Vronsky commented, nearly bursting with amusement.

"Hmm . . ." commented Oblonsky, staring after Alyosha. "I don't know what came over the lad; he's usually very reserved." Shaking his head, he returned his attention to the doppelganger. "But, I suppose, it's to be expected . . . given the recent incident. It seems to have everyone quite frazzled."

"Incident? What incident is that?"

"They say the old pawnbroker woman was murdered," said Oblonsky. "Apparently her skull was smashed in with an axe!"

"Well, it wasn't me!" replied the Second Vronsky, defensively. "I was nowhere near there last night!"

"But . . ." Oblonsky began questioningly, ". . . I didn't say where it happened. Or when, for that matter . . ."

"Hmm . . . just as well, really," said the doppelganger, looking randomly about and patting at his pockets as if in search of some elusive object. "Probably not even relevant."

"Here, now!" Oblonsky demanded. "You're behaving very mysteriously—even for you! Tell me how you knew!"

"Well . . ." the Second Vronsky exclaimed, as if completely exasperated, ". . . of course it had to have happened last night, because if it had happened earlier I would have surely heard about it before now . . ."

"Yes," Oblonsky agreed grudgingly. "There is that . . ."

"And, further, I would assume you were speaking of the pawnbroker woman who lives several streets over from me . . . I mean, if it hadn't been a local crime, why would you be all worked up over it? Why would you think I might even be interested?"

"Ah, well, you make a good point, I suppose," Oblonsky replied. "I'm sorry if—"

Beginning to feel rather cocky—and (perhaps) just the slightest bit *cockney*— the Second Vronsky interrupted, "So there you go—obviously it couldn' o' been me then what offed the ol' lady . . . 'cause, like I said, I weren' nowhere near there last night . . ."

"I should say! It's absolutely preposterous to even suggest you would be guilty of the crime!" Oblonsky cried, shocked. "I certainly never meant to imply anything of the sort!"

"Well, awright then," the Second Vronsky said, leaning casually with his back against the wall they were beside and absently stroking his beard in a very superior manner. "So who done it then, eh? If you'll pardon the pun—who do you think might 'ave been on hand when the ol' lady *bought* it?. . . What say there, guv'na? What do the blokes on the street say?"

"'Blokes'?!" A doubting look again crossed Oblonsky's face. "You're being rather odd again, Vronsky . . . and whom do you think you're calling 'guv'na'?" he asked.

"Say, I can't exactly go 'round calling folk 'boyar' now, can I? I'd get me faced bashed in, I would!" Suddenly realizing he had, indeed, been acting and sounding peculiarly, the Second Vronsky made an extra effort toward adhering to a more 'Vronsky-ish' demeanor. "Er . . . that is . . . merely having a bit of fun with you!" He laughed and tried to make it sound light-hearted, but it came across as unnatural.

"I don't know . . ." said Oblonsky, unconvinced. "You just don't at all seem yourself today . . ."

"Oh, really?" the doppelganger replied, tersely. "Then whom do you suppose I am—*exactly?!. . .*"

"Now, now, here, here," Oblonsky began, trying to placate the Second Vronsky. "No cause to get upset; I meant no harm, you realize—it's just you're behaving rather . . . erratically? Or . . ."

"Ye-e-ss?!" the Second Vronsky prompted through gritted teeth, working for all he was worth to restrain his anger.

"Well . . . sort of weird . . ."

"Oh!" Suddenly the doppelganger's anger drained away as he realized he was not, after all, found out. *"But, of course,"* he thought to himself, laughing, *"he is a bulging, old fool, so overflowing with innocuousness that it seeps out his ear and drips down the side of his face—as if a pimple on his brain has spurted its pus right out the side of his head! If anyone is to discover I'm not me—or at least not the me they suppose me to be—certainly it would not be him!. . ."* And he went on laughing until he realized quite some time had passed and Oblonsky was staring at him with an expression akin to terror.

"Ah, yes," the Second Vronsky said, smiling and completely at ease again. "I see now. But I'd nearly forgotten! I saw a man—when was that?. . . where was I?. . . oh, but it doesn't matter!—and he could have been your twin! He had the same face, same balding pate and squinty eyes and bulbous nose; the same oblongish form; he used the same expressions and gestures, the same body language; even his voice seemed completely identical to—"

"Yes? Yes?" Oblonsky begged, his eyes wide with wonder. "Do go on!"

"No, no . . . nevermind," said the Second Vronsky, waving it all away. "I remember now—I was thinking of when last we met. My apologies, I'm sure . . . but now, of course, you can see how one might seem other than you have previously taken him—even if the only difference lies in how similar he seems to himself. And perhaps on that previous occasion it was you who was not himself, and thus my confusion . . ."

"Yes . . ." Oblonsky agreed, crestfallen to learn he did not, after all, have a double. "Yes, I see your point . . ."

"I really don't see why people are always seeming to insist that it's the other person who isn't himself. Why are they forever unable to see that sometimes it is they who aren't themselves? Who they are, then, I have no idea—and I suppose it isn't any of my business anyway—but it shouldn't have to mean I have to brunt the blame of it all . . . I mean—"

"Oh, all right already!" erupted Oblonsky. "I'm sorry, and I didn't mean anything by it! At least now I know it really is you—you frustrating, bothersome man, you!"

"Hmf! Well . . ." the Second Vronsky replied aghast, "you're certainly in a mood today . . ." Oblonsky's mouth dropped open at the audacious accusation, but before he could respond, the doppelganger's tone shifted once again. "Hey, you don't have any pastries on you, do you? I could really go for some pastries!"

Chapter Nine

By the time of their return from Italy, Vronsky felt happier and more relaxed than he ever had before . . . which he knew to be misleading, owing to the fact that the majority of the happiest and most relaxed occasions in his life were drug or alcohol induced—simply a matter of not remembering, really. . .

Anna, on the other hand, was not fairing so well. To Vronsky it seemed as if she could be perfectly happy, smiling and laughing and singing one moment, and the next she was flustered and trembling and overcome with tears. At first he felt she must be going mad, but then he realized he had seen the same behavior in any number of women before—if not to the same extremes—and so he tried to ignore her "attacks" (as he called them) as best he could, giving her the space he knew he would want should he ever begin to act as if he were going mad . . .

Although, in the beginning, Anna had thought her trip abroad with Vronsky would, indeed, provide the opportunity to build a basis for their love, thus allowing a certain peace of mind for her despite the unusual circumstances involved—namely her marriage to Karenin—but after a week or so, when the initial excitement of 'being away' had worn thin, she discovered she felt worse than ever. Given her rigidly Orthodox upbringing, she simply could not adopt Vronsky's view that, because her husband was not as attentive or affectionate as she might like, he was undeserving of her—thus making her relationship with Vronsky acceptable. The bond of marriage was sacred, and while in Italy Anna still felt overwrought with guilt by the affair . . . now she felt as if she had abandoned her husband as well.

When, upon their return to Russia, Anna told Vronsky perhaps what she needed was some time to herself, he felt really rather hurt . . . ultimately resolved if such was what she truly needed for her own well-being, he would support her decision—if what Anna wanted most from him right now was his absence, then he would oblige her request . . . (he neglected to mention how her incessant crying was beginning to rattle his nerves, and he could really use a break away from her as well . . .). But when Anna announced her intention to stay with Kitty and Levin—who had married while Anna and Vronsky were away—at their country estate, Vronsky almost changed his mind about not accompanying her . . . remembering the pertness of Kitty's breasts—and somehow aroused even further by the knowledge she was now someone's wife—Vronsky declared a purposed interest in again seeing Levin. Anna, however, pointed out there could be no acceptable way to explain her and Vronsky's presence together—especially given Vronsky had supposedly gone to St. Petersburg—and, thus, when Anna left the train to travel by carriage the rest of the way to Levin's estate, Vronsky grudgingly continued on toward Moscow . . .

"Oh, I simply adore the country now," Kitty said, pouring Anna a cup of tea, "but when Levin and I first married, I found it simply dreadful!"

"I understand completely," replied Anna meekly as she accepted the cup with a timid smile. They were sitting in a little garden filled with beautiful flowers, overlooking a duck pond, and the sun was shining down on them, warm and bright . . . Anna was trying to relax and not think or feel anything, but it was taking a little while for her tensions to slip away, even in such a delightfully serene setting. "When I first arrived in Italy, we—that is I—stayed in a villa outside the city, and it was just so quiet and . . . and lonely, I guess . . ."

"Yes, yes!" Kitty exclaimed. "That's exactly how it felt. But I suppose I got used to it quickly enough."

"But you should have seen her the first week or so," added Levin, with a snort. "She had no idea what to do with herself—why she didn't know whether to shit or go blind!"

"It's true, darling," Kitty replied, smiling. "So true . . . but now that I've made this my home, I don't miss the noise and the bustle and the dirt of Moscow—although, I must admit, I do long for the societal functions that we're just too far away to regularly attend. And I do sometimes wish for someone with whom I can just sit and chat . . ." Jumping up out of her chair, she leaned down to give Anna a hug. "Oh, Anna! I'm so very happy you've stopped by to visit us! And here I've just been gaggling away like an old goose the whole time—now, you simply must tell me all about your holiday abroad!"

"Oh, well . . . I . . . that is—" Anna faltered, thrown off by the other woman's enthusiasm.

"Holy shit, Kitty," Levin said, laughing, as he peeled his wife off their guest and set her gently back into her chair. "Let the poor woman breathe; you've got her so flustered she probably can't even find her tongue! She just got here this morning—let her rest . . ."

"No, no," Anna assured them. "I'm fine, really . . . I just—"

"Well, shit in a kettle and call it stew!" Levin growled, looking across the yard to where half a dozen serfs lay relaxing on a hay wagon. "If those lazy shit-holes don't get off their slacker asses and get that hay in by nightfall, sure as shit I'm going to rip off each and every one of their heads and shit right down their stinking necks!" Turning back to Anna and Kitty, Levin bowed slightly, with no sign whatsoever of the angry outburst of but a second earlier, and said smiling, "If you ladies will excuse me—duty calls . . ."

"My goodness, Kitty!" Anna declared, after he had gone. "Is he all right? He seems so different than I remember . . . so volatile—and vulgarly so!"

"Oh, yes . . ." Kitty replied hazily, a dreamy smile on her lips. "He's so rugged that way . . . very different than in the city; to be completely honest, I don't think he even realizes . . . probably the fresh country air . . ."

With a sigh, Kitty shook her head—as if clearing her thoughts upon waking from a particularly sordid sort of dream—and continued, "But at any rate, Anna, it really is so very wonderful to see you. And—oh!—the happenings that have been going on in Moscow while you were away!"

"What sort of happenings?" Anna asked, anxious to catch up on the gossip back home.

"Well, you know it has to be something especially good—or, rather, especially *bad*—for us to hear about it way out here," said Kitty with a kind of conspiratorial lowering of her voice, despite there being no one around to hear. "The whole city is talking about him—I shouldn't wonder the whole country! My goodness!"

"Who?" demanded Anna. "Who is everyone talking about?"

"Why, your friend, that Vronsky character," Kitty replied. "That horrible, horrible, *delightful* man who has been hanging around recently . . ."

Anna's heart stopped and her eyes grew wide. "How—" She didn't know where to begin. Had someone found out about her and Vronsky? Did they know he had been with her in Italy? . . . "I mean, what exactly have they been saying about Mr. Vronsky?"

"Easier to tell you what they haven't been saying, I would think," Kitty said with a laugh; her eyes were glazed over now in full gossip-mode and she didn't even notice how pale and rigid Anna had become. "For the last month—since around the time you left for your holiday, I would say— he's been out carousing; there seems no end to the mischief he's been getting into."

"But—" *But he was with me*, she had been about to say, but Anna caught herself in time. "But he had said he was going to Petersburg on business . . ."

"Oh, yes, well, apparently that was cancelled—or perhaps he simply quit his job, I really don't know. He's certainly kept busy enough as it is, with his nights occupied wandering from tavern to tavern and from club to club—practically swimming in vodka (and lord knows what else!) by the sound of it; and vandalism, destroying property, items that turn up missing after he's been there—though nothing substantial enough to lead to an arrest . . . he's very clever about that . . . and then of course there are the women—a different one every night . . . sometimes two or three hanging all over him at once . . ." Kitty cringed and with a shiver—seeming not entirely convincing about it—she commented, "Disgusting!"

Anna was distraught—confused, astonished, angry but wondering if she had any right to be angry because all that Kitty was saying was completely impossible, and wondering if she was perhaps going mad after all . . . a myriad of emotions passed through her, none of them taking hold, but merely smacking her boldly in the back of the head when she was turned away, and then when she whirled to confront it, whisking off to avoid being captured. A multitude of thoughts flitted through her mind, an endless barrage of possible explanations—each one more preposterous than the last . . .

"I have to go!" Anna cried, leaping from her chair and pacing frantically about.

Kitty, finally noticing Anna's dithered condition, rose to embrace her friend. "Anna, dear Anna! What do you mean? You've only just arrived! Are you all right?"

"Yes—no! I don't know!" Anna slumped weakly against Kitty. "I don't know anything at all . . . but I have to return to Moscow—I must leave at once!"

Before Kitty could reply, Anna broke away and ran toward the house to prepare for her journey home . . .

Chapter Ten

Oblonsky found the Second Vronsky in a tavern with a woman—whom Oblonsky thought looked like a Cossack whore—on his lap and a German to his left. Too angry to even speak, Oblonsky merely hovered over their table glowering and clenching and unclenching his fists.

"Oblonsky, my friend," the doppelganger declared, joyously. "Have you brought any pastries with you? I would truly love a pastry just now!"

"Oh!" cried the woman perched on his lap. "I love pastries! Especially the crème filled with chocolate frosting!"

Ignoring her, Oblonsky finally found his voice. "You are just evil!" he growled at the Second Vronsky in a restrained shout.

"You say that as if it were a bad thing . . ." the German commented, an intrigued eyebrow arched inquisitively.

"But who am I?" the doppelganger cried out suddenly, slapping himself soundly on the forehead. "*(But where are you?)* You have yet to meet my companions . . . this," he said, indicating the German, "is the esteemed Dr. Schopenhauer, visiting from France."

"*Deutschland,*" Schopenhauer corrected him.

"*Gesundheit,*" replied the woman and Oblonsky at once.

"From Le Havre, wasn't it?" continued the Second Vronsky.

"Danzig," Schopenhauer replied, slurping from his beer.

"Ah, ha! I knew it!" He tapped a forefinger to his head, adding, "I've got a mind like a steel sieve . . . and this delicious morsel . . ." he said, holding the woman as if to squeeze at the very essence of her with every fiber of his being, ". . . is the beautiful gypsy princess, Katerina!"

The woman giggled, slapping the Second Vronsky playfully in the shoulder. "My name's Tess!"

"Enough of this . . . frivolity!" Oblonsky sputtered angrily, ignoring both the German and the woman, focusing directly on the doppelganger. "I know you've corrupted my sister—you no doubt are the cause of this illness that has taken her abroad—but she told me to keep to my own business, and I fully intended to do so. However, I shall not—absolutely *can*not—stand by and watch you destroy her in this fashion by taking up with this common, little tramp and breaking Anna's heart! Your carrying on about town since she's been gone is the talk of all of Moscow; I demand that it stop this instant and that you begin acting like a proper gentleman!"

The doppelganger frowned, weaving back and forth slightly, as if he might have fallen drunkenly from his chair had it not been for Tess holding him down.

After a moment or two of silence—which Oblonsky took as quiet consideration of all he'd said—the Second Vronsky commented, "You seem tense, Obbie; you should stay for a while and share some vodka with us . . ." Turning to Schopenhauer, he continued, "what do you think, Doc?"

"*Nein, danka*," the German replied. "I'll stick with my beer."

Laughing, the Second Vronsky turned back to Oblonsky. "Isn't he great! These Germans are *funny!* Always with their beer instead of vodka . . . they have to drink ten times more of it to feel anything at all!"

"Actually," Schopenhauer corrected him, as they clinked glasses together in salute, "to feel *nothing!*"

With a sigh of exasperation, Oblonsky insisted, "Now, Vronsky, I truly mean it—I so dislike any sort of confrontation, but if you refuse to be true to Anna, I shall have to ask you to step outside . . ."

"Why?" asked the Second Vronsky, dubiously. "What's out there?"

"*Nein, nein,*" said Schopenhauer, leaning in as if to whisper in the Second Vronsky's ear, though not at all lowering his voice; "I believe he intends to challenge you as a gentleman."

"A duel?"

Schopenhauer shook his head. "I don't think quite so extravagant as that . . ."

"A *brawl* then!?!"

"*Ja,* so it would seem."

"But . . ." the Second Vronsky frowned, unable to get his mind around the idea. ". . . I'd kick his ass . . ."

"Indubitably," Schopenhauer agreed. "Let me see what I can do with him." Taking a long draft from his beer, he turned his attention toward the still fuming Oblonsky. "My good sir—"

"I am not your good anything!" Oblonsky retorted hotly.

"I guess that would make you a *good for nothing!*" Tess cried out cheerfully, and then almost giggled herself onto the floor.

"As you say, as you say," Schopenhauer said, oblivious to the woman's interjection. "But let me put to you the question: Are not all one? And what I mean by this is, are not all things that we can perceive through the senses created of the same matter?"

Confused, Oblonsky stepped back from his attack. "Well, I suppose . . ." he agreed, though he hadn't a clue what the German was talking about.

"Good, good," Schopenhauer nodded approvingly. To the Second Vronsky, he added, "This one,"—he indicated Oblonsky—"he is not so dumb as you have said."

"*What*?!" Oblonsky demanded, his anger again exploding forth. "How dare you—"

"*Ach*! Tush, tush . . ." Schopenhauer waved away the other's objection. "And so, if we have surmised correctly that all are one—and we have, have we not? You have admitted it yourself—then we may deduce that this woman Tess, who perches now so prettily upon the lap of our friend Vronsky, is, indeed, your sister Anna, whom we all adore so well *(though, I must admit, I have yet to meet her . . . even so, I feel no small amount of compassion for the woman in the mere anticipation of one day making her acquaintance . . .)* And, if all are now perched so prettily—"

"All right, okay," the Second Vronsky interrupted, laughing. "Now you're just babbling, you silly, German bastard! Can't you—"

"Ah-ah-ah! Never say 'Kant'!"

"Sorry . . . I forgot . . ." apologized the doppelganger, rolling his eyes. "*Couldn't* you wrap things up here?"

"As you say," Schopenhauer conceded, doffing a hat he wasn't wearing. "Thusly, if all are one, and this girl here is that other girl there (wherever she is now), then all girls are this one, and this one, all girls—and all people, whether female or male . . . so it could be said, as people ourselves, that we are this girl! And thus we are Anna!"

"Oh, dear . . ." Oblonsky mumbled, sinking shocked into a chair.

"Now you're just completely over the edge, Doc," the Second Vronsky said, suppressing a shiver of revulsion. "I mean, to each their own, and all that—but leave me out of it!"

Schopenhauer began rising to his feet, a gleam of inspiration in his eyes. "And not just humans, but animals of all types! Everything is Anna! *Anna is Everything!*"

Oblonsky leaned in toward Vronsky's double. "Is there any way to shut him down?"

"I'm not sure," the doppelganger admitted. "Hey, Doc! You need another beer?"

"Ah!" Schopenhauer sighed, retaking his seat. "*Ja, ja*, a beer would be *wunderbar!*"

"So then, Oblonsky," began the Second Vronsky, "are we all right again, or do you still want to take me outside?"

Oblonsky poured a glass of vodka for himself, drinking it in down in one gulp. Hanging his head in his hands, he groaned, "I am so confused . . ."

"This is true," Schopenhauer agreed, nodding knowingly. "For such is life: Inconsequence, futility, confusion . . . and then there is death . . ."

Vronsky Vronsky Vronsky Vronsky returned to his apartment in the wee hours of the morning. Tess hung heavily from his left arm, dragging listlessly alongside him, occasionally almost becoming alert enough to mumble something incoherent before complete unconsciousness once again reclaimed her. After two solid weeks of incessant drinking and debauchery, he didn't feel as if he were in much better condition . . . (Even so, he could not help but chuckle to think of poor Oblonsky—unaccustomed as he was to the endeavors they had lead him through in a mere two days . . . he would be lucky to wake up at all!)

Depositing Tess unceremoniously in a chair beside the door, the Second Vronsky began pulling off his clothes as he trudged across the room to his bed. He had managed to remove his right shoe, as well as the corresponding leg of his pants, his jacket, and for the most part his shirt—which he had tried to take off over his head without undoing any of the buttons. Upon falling ungracefully onto the bed, the shirt still wrapped about his head with one arm yet held captive, he felt he had been thorough enough in his ambition of disrobing and promptly passed out . . . little wonder, in such a state, he was completely oblivious to the other man in his bed . . .

Chapter Eleven

Vronsky awoke to the jostling of another climbing into bed beside him. At first intrigued at the prospect of who it might be—and amused he seemed to have forgotten whom he had brought home with him—he suddenly realized he could not have brought anyone home . . . indeed, he had not gone carousing at all, but had returned straight to his apartment upon reaching the Moscow train station.

Leaping to his feet, Vronsky tore the blankets from the figure beside him; the other man began to struggle in return, and soon the two of them were but a tangle of limbs and blankets and pillows, wrangling across the floor.

"Who?!" Vronsky demanded, tearing free from the melee. "Who are you? What are you doing here? I think it only fair to warn you, I—"

Lifting the other to his feet and pulling away the blanket and shirt caught around the man's head, Vronsky was stunned into silence as he was confronted by the visage of his own face. The likeness was beyond amazing—it was veritably perfect . . . as if looking into a mirror . . .

The Second Vronsky returned the stare, initially equally startled, but—as he was at least aware of the actual number of Vronskys currently at large—he recovered quickly.

"Well, well," the double said, beginning to chuckle, "look who's finally home!"

Before Vronsky could summon the clarity of thought to utter a reply, there was a reticent tapping at the door; both he and his double turned to see Oblonsky's clerk, Alyosha, peek his head in.

"Begging your pardon, Mr. Vronsky," Alyosha apologized, coming all the way into the room and nearly tripping over Tess where she lay draped over her chair; "I'm certainly very sorry, you understand, for calling so

124

early—and then unannounced yet—but I'm concerned over Mr. Oblonsky, you see, and I thought—" Alyosha abruptly halted as the realization he was speaking to two Vronskys caught up to him; up until that point he had been completely unaware due to his own discomfort and nervousness.

Turning pale, Alyosha muttered, "Oh, dear!" and he began backing toward the door. His eyes darting madly back and forth between the two men, he failed to even notice as he fell into the lap of the unconscious Tess.

The doppelganger resumed his chuckling. "How very awkward for us all, don't you think?" he said, crossing the room to close the door. "I doubt either of you will mind if we keep all this amongst ourselves? It seems the sort of thing to put some people off . . ."

"What's going on here?" demanded Vronsky, at last rediscovering his voice. He took half a step toward his double, but then cautiously shied away, instead confronting Alyosha, whom, he guessed, seemed innocuous enough. "Tell me now—who are all of you and what do you want here?" He picked Alyosha up by the lapels of his jacket and began shaking him, though never taking his eyes from the second Vronsky for even a moment. "Answer me!"

Alyosha trembled with fear, trying to free himself from Vronsky's clutches—but his fear was quickly replaced by relief as his hands came into contact with Vronsky's; becoming veritably elated, he began grabbing and grasping and grappling all over his accoster, feeling his arms and shoulders and face and hair.

"You're not evil!" Alyosha cried. "I can't express how terrified I was to come here—after what happened when last we met . . ." He shivered at the mere remembrance of the episode.

"All right, all right, just knock it off!" said Vronsky, slapping the other man's groping hands away. "What in the hell are you talking about?!"

"But that's just it!" Alyosha replied, joyously. "Not in Hell at all . . . I thought you an apparition—perhaps even a demon! . . . but now I sense I was wrong, for there is no evil in you at all!"

Vronsky sighed, shaking his head in disbelief. "Well, good—I'm glad we've got *that* settled . . . put your mind at ease then, did I?"

"Oh, yes—very much so!"

"Good, good . . . although, given I've never laid eyes on you before now, and there's another me standing right over there—" He gestured toward the doppelganger, who waved at Alyosha, flashing a large, toothy grin. "—I don't believe I would be incorrect in conjecturing that this is your apparition . . ."

Alyosha quietly returned to trembling and growing ever more pale.

"Yes, well, there you have it," said the Second Vronsky, seeming wholly amused by the entire spectacle. "Or, rather, you've almost got it . . . as you can see," he continued, pounding on the wall with his fist and stomping on the floor with his foot, "I'm a bit too substantial to be a mere phantasm."

"A demon!" Alyosha squeaked, seeming to nearly swallow his throat.

"Hmm . . . more or less, I suppose . . ."

"So then why do you look like me?" Vronsky asked.

"Well, because I'm your evil doppelganger, of course . . ." the Second Vronsky replied, seeming dumbfounded the answer hadn't been completely apparent.

"Ah, yes—how silly of me!" said Vronsky, forcing an embarrassed sort of laugh. "I'm sorry, but could you excuse us for just a moment?"

"Yes, of course," the double said agreeably, and sat down in Tess's lap to play with her lips while Vronsky led Alyosha to the other side of the room.

"Now then," began Vronsky, speaking in very low tones so as not to be overheard, "this is all just a bit new to me—I've never actually run into any demons when I hadn't been drinking . . . (and those when I had been generally turned out to be unfortunate misunderstandings after I'd sobered up) . . . but that's neither here nor there—as you seem like a monkly sort of a fellow—"

Alyosha regained a flush of color to his cheeks, as, somewhat exasperated, he interjected, "Why does everyone keep saying that?"

"But you are, aren't you?"

". . . yes, I suppose so . . ." Alyosha agreed reluctantly. "Though that's not what we call it . . ."

Vronsky waved away Alyosha's complaint. "The point is, do you know how to deal with this other me?"

"Well," Alyosha replied, after a brief moment to collect his thoughts; "he doesn't seem to be an all-out sort of a demon—if you take my meaning—but he does imply an underlying essence of evil as his source of being...so I would imagine if we could somehow remove him from that evil source, it should destroy him . . ."

"So we must tear away the foundation of his existence? . . ." mused Vronsky aloud, trying to clarify the situation. "By convincing him there is no evil!"

Alyosha was aghast. "No evil?! But the ramifications . . ."

"Damn the ramifications!" Vronsky insisted. "Do you think there's a chance?"

"Well, I would presume whatever beliefs held by you—whom the demon has modeled itself after—should hold a certain influence over it . . ." Alyosha shrugged uncomfortably. "Though we really haven't gotten as far as demonic exorcism at the seminary yet . . ."

A course of action decided, Vronsky and Alyosha returned to the doppelganger.

"You know, what really should be asked . . ." began Alyosha pontifically before Vronsky could speak, ". . . is, if in the same position I now find myself, what would Jesus do?"

"Ha!" the double laughed mirthlessly, replacing Tess's tongue in her mouth and returning his attention to Vronsky and Alyosha. "What, indeed! No doubt he'd do exactly as he did the last time—tuck his halo between his legs and run . . ."

"Oh!" Alyosha exclaimed, as if he had been physically struck. "It wasn't like that at all!" he returned, indignantly.

"Here he is preaching the 'Word' of the 'Lord God Almighty'— pretty boring stint, I'd say—and he sees how pointless it all is, so he gives himself over to the Romans to save himself from the futility of the rest of his life . . . he, himself, was the only one your 'Savior' was saving!"

"But, He . . . He—but . . .!"

"Here, here," said Vronsky, setting the sputtering Alyosha off to the side. "Maybe I'd better handle this . . . you know, um . . . well, *you there*—" he said, uncertain as to what to call the creature. "There's one thing that bothers me—you say you are an 'evil' doppelganger of me?"

"Hmm, yes, that's right."

"But how can that be? To say you are a creature of evil would mean there would have to be some sort of ultimate source of evil in the universe . . ."

"Yes . . ." the double replied, uncertain where Vronsky was headed.

"And there isn't."

The Second Vronsky frowned for half a second before bursting into laughter. "I might have known you'd try something like this! It's because of this very attitude you're putting forth now that has made my job so very difficult—you're rather a tough act to follow, you know! You barely give a fellow any room to maneuver . . ."

Now it was Vronsky's turn to frown. "What?!" he demanded, irritably. "Just what the hell is that supposed to mean?!"

"Oh, just that you yourself can be quite the nasty bastard at times, as well . . ."

Vronsky relaxed, smiling. "Oh, yes . . . *that* . . ."

"But don't doubt for a minute that I was successful in my endeavors," the doppelganger went on. "I've stolen from friends, abused children, molested women, beaten men, lied to everyone, and corrupted anyone I could—I, sir, am evil!"

"But I've done all those things," Vronsky countered, "and I'm not evil . . ."

"Oh—but wait!" the Second Vronsky cried, excitedly. "I killed a woman!"

"You did *what?!*" Vronsky and Alyosha replied together.

"I committed murder," the double replied, proudly. "An old woman—I just bashed in her skull with an axe and took all her money!" He laughed, feeling he had proven his point. "So I guess I'm just evil after all . . ."

"The old pawnbroker . . ." Alyosha muttered, sickened.

"Which one?" Vronsky asked. "That old hag up the street here?"

"What difference does it make who she was?" the Second Vronsky countered, defensively. "Murder is evil!"

"Well, yes and no . . ." replied Vronsky. ". . . in an absolutist sort of sense I would have to agree—but if it's the old shrew I'm thinking of . . . well, I've thought of doing her in several times myself—always figured it would be doing the world a favor, really . . ."

"Yes, you've *thought* about it," countered the doppelganger; "but I've done something about it—and not in an effort to improve the world, or anything so sentimental as that, but—"

"Yes, yes, let me guess," Vronsky interrupted; "'just to watch her die'. . ."

A maniacal twinkle in his eye, the double grinned. "No—I didn't even need that much reason . . ."

Alyosha whimpered.

"And anyway," the Second Vronsky continued, "regardless of what you would or would not do, you've said it yourself—you behave with the impetus of good intentions; you exercise or endorse unsavory actions—such as justifiable murder to rid others of a bothersome old crone—in an effort toward making the world a better place"

"So intent is relevant?" asked Vronsky, grasping at the opportunity his other had presented. "There aren't good actions and evil actions—it's all in the underlying purpose inducing the action?"

"Yes, of course . . ."

"Then the universe is subjective, and there can be no basis for evil because it's all in how we perceive and interpret it; the essence of existence, therefore, is neutral!"

"But . . ." the doppelganger faltered momentarily as he scratched at his neck and tried to ignore the muscle spasm that had suddenly erupted in his cheek. "But what about the Grand Design!" he declared after a moment. "What about the schemes and plottings of the gods!"

"You're contradicting yourself now," Vronsky returned. "Any sort of supernatural confluence with human endeavors—such as destiny or fate—implies a dominance over will, which would make the intentions of any action completely irrelevant; any judgment made concerning the behavior enacted by a given individual would be meaningless, as the individual could only ever be the innocent dupe of the fanciful whims of some god. And, of course, if such were the case, there could be no sin—and so there would still be no evil!"

"Well . . . that seems a bit far-flung," retorted the double, seeming not entirely convinced. The itch on his neck that he continued to scratch unconsciously away at seemed to be spreading—along with the muscle spasm in his cheek—creating a deep crimson throbbing across his upper torso. Ignoring it, he commented, *"Yo tengo un lapis; mi lapis es amarillo!"*

Vronsky exchanged a questioning glance with Alyosha. "I think it's working . . ." Keeping on the offensive, Vronsky continued, "Thusly, whereas in an objective universe—in which any manner of absolutes might exist—in a subjective universe, all 'things' are relative to the ideas and beliefs deduced from the senses of all others existing in the immediately perceivable vicinity . . ."

"Is it warm in here, or is it just me?" the Second Vronsky asked, his very flesh roiling about as if swarms of bees crawled about below the skin. Smoke began seeping from his ears and nose, and his frenzied scratching had become a violent tearing, producing a syrupy, blackish-red goop that dripped all down the front of him. "Perhaps if we might just open a window or something?"

". . . and, because you have admitted to being a creature whose existence is based entirely on a penultimate force of evil," Vronsky went on, ignoring—yet privately reveling in—his double's discomfort, "and I have no reason to doubt your belief in the matter—do you, sir?"

"I have no doubt," Alyosha agreed.

"Well, then we must affirm with absolute certainty, as we are all in agreement—"

"*Don't . . . say it!*" pleaded the Second Vronsky—really not at all a complete second anymore, so much as about three-quarters again of a Vronsky—one of its eyes melting and running, as a tear, down its blistering cheek; it was now on its knees, thrashing about convulsively, rivers of the syrupy goop running down to form a steaming pool of putrescence all around it.

"—because you are a subjective being of objective evil in a universe which does not allow for the possibility of an objective evil," blurted Vronsky, "you are thus a complete paradox of being and therefore cannot rightly exist!"

The doppelganger tried to reply, yet being predominantly liquid—and even that rapidly evaporating into a smoky, fetid, foot-like stench—all it could muster was a sort of pathetic gurgling. As the brackish wisps of the creature's remains permeated the room, the air seemed to come alive as if a current of electricity coursed through it—or as if a soul were clinging desperately to its corporeal existence, yet was being adamantly and inexorably pulled ever away—

And then it was gone.

Chapter Twelve

Even as the last electrical vestiges of Vronsky's double faded away, Tess began stretching and groaning herself awake.

Feeling buoyed by his victory over the doppelganger, Vronsky walked over to her with the intention of introducing himself. "Ah, and even as the sun rises," he said, taking her hand, "so, too, does this brilliant vision before us . . ." Bestowing a light kiss upon her beauteous knucklage, he hesitated, frowning; licking his lips and then outright tasting her hand, he asked, "What *is* that?"

Tasting it herself, Tess replied, "Custard . . ." As she answered, she seemed to come fully awake, and seeing it was Vronsky to whom she spoke, she rose and cuddled up to him, all slinky like an overly affectionate cat. "Good morning, lover," she growled, wrapping herself around him where he stood. "You were *wonderful* last night . . ."

"Yes, well, I'm sorry, my dear, but—"

Before Vronsky could try to explain that nothing had happened, Anna walked into the apartment.

"'Wonderful'?!" she demanded, standing stiffly, her entire body an accusation. She looked as if she wanted to cry, and the only way of not doing so was by embracing her anger. "What does she mean, Vronsky, that you were '*wonderful*'?!"

"Anna, darling!" Vronsky replied, disentangling himself from Tess and hurrying over to Anna. "What a joyous surprise! I was just—"

"Yes, yes, I see what you were *just*!" Anna returned, coldly. "So it's all true then—everything Kitty told me . . . I don't know how it's possible, but—oh, Vronsky!" she cried, breaking down and crumpling into his arms. "How could you?!"

"Well, as I was about to explain—"

"Oh! As if I could believe anything you tell me anymore!" she said, sobbing, frustrated, pounding her fists on his chest.

"Yes, well . . . there is that . . ." Vronsky grudgingly had to agree. "But I have a witness this time!" he announced, remembering Alyosha, who now sat quiet and contemplative and seemingly completely unaware of the scene before him. "Surely you'll believe the word of a scholarly, religious man? Tell her, Alyosha, my friend—tell them both—I've done nothing wrong!"

"Hmm?" Alyosha replied, absently, after half a moment. "Oh, I do apologize, Mr. Vronsky; I'm feeling a bit . . . distracted, is all . . . I can't help but wonder, if—as we expressed to dispel the demon that had stolen your image—there is no ultimate source of evil in the world, can there then be any ultimate source of good?"

Vronsky slumped dejectedly. "Oh, bloody hell . . ." he swore.

"I mean," Alyosha continued, "my belief in the Almighty is the very foundation of my life—of my *being* . . . and what the creature said of the Savior—if it's true, what does that make of my life? If—"

"This is no time for a religious crisis!" Vronsky exploded. "It was meant to convince my double—not you!"

Startled by Vronsky's outburst, Tess began hacking and coughing violently, as if she had swallowed a particularly uncooperative bit of something that didn't entirely want to go down all the way—such as, perhaps, her tongue. When she had finished, she wiped her nose on the sleeve of her dress and asked, "Is anyone else interested in getting some breakfast?"

"There are some pastries here on the table," said Alyosha, quickly scurrying over to offer the tray to her. Seeing the way her bosom had heaved—nearly seductively, he thought—during her coughing fit, presented Alyosha with feelings he had, in the past, left unexplored . . .

"I can't stand the lies anymore, Vronsky," Anna declared, turning to leave. "I can't live with all the deceit and—"

As she got to the door, two figures stumbled in, blocking her escape.

"Anna!" Oblonsky declared, drawing her into his arms and embracing her in an almost un-brotherly manner. "It's glorious to have you home, sister dear!"

"My god!" Anna cried in shock, pulling away. "You're drunk?!"

"Oh, indeed, indeed," he replied, trying to act very sober and somber, but unable to pull it off due to the way he weaved and wavered in merely trying to stand there. With a hiccup, he went on, "And this is my associate, the esteemed Dr. Schopenhauer . . ."

"Ah!" said Schopenhauer; "it is truly a delight to meet you . . ." To Oblonsky, he asked, "Is this the one, then, with all the fuss?"

"That's right," Oblonsky answered.

Turning back to Anna, the German wagged a finger antagonizingly under her nose and becoming quite surly, said, "So it's all about *you*, then, is it?!"

"Well, I don't know what this is all about," began Vronsky, stepping between Anna and the German—but that was as far as he got . . .

"Alyosha!" Oblonsky shouted; he rushed over to the young man, embracing him, as he had Anna, in a very un-brotherly manner, and said, "It's glorious to have you home, sister dear!" Oblonsky began humming to himself and dancing with Alyosha, who was oblivious to the other man's advances, fixated as he was on the décolletage of Tess's dress.

Vronsky again stepped forward in an attempt to restore order, but was interrupted as Lolita—from his summer by the sea—entered, leading along a young Spaniard.

"Oh! There you are, Vronsky Vronsky!" she declared with overly dramatic, exasperated relief. She spoke with that very superior tone of a young person trying to seem older than she truly was. "I've been looking just everywhere for you . . ."

"Well, there's the problem then, darling," Vronsky replied, masking his confusion at her appearance with nonchalance. "I wasn't everywhere—I was here . . ."

"Hmm . . . yes," she agreed, taking in the growing assemblage that filled the room. "As it seems everyone else was, as well . . ."

"*Ja! Ja!*" Schopenhauer interjected excitedly, running over to Lolita, but pointing his yet waggling finger back at Anna. "This is the one—she is *everyone!* We are all she! And so, Oblonsky?"

"*If I were a cherry tomato, my love, and you were a dollop of crème* . . ." Oblonsky sang, ignoring the German.

"Yes, well . . . how very droll . . ." commented Lolita. "But, at any rate, Vronsky Vronsky, I have simply horrid news for you, and I've no doubt it will just completely undo you—but there's no good avoiding it . . . best to just come right out with it, so here it is—I shan't hold back—"

"Could you not hold back a little more quickly, my dear . . ." Vronsky prompted her, kicking away Alyosha, who was trying to lick Lolita's knee-pit.

"Hmm . . . yes, well, very well, then, I suppose . . . you see, I don't love you anymore! There—I've said it, it's out! I'm sorry, Vronsky Vronsky, dear, but I just don't love you, and so I'm running away with Manuel . . ."

"Ah, ha!" Vronsky cried, grabbing the hand of the Spaniard beside her and shaking it vigorously. "So *you* are Manuel! Well, this is, indeed, a pleasure!"

Noting Vronsky's distraction, Anna again made for the door—yet was once more intercepted.

"Kitty!" Anna declared, surprised—for such was who now stood before her, accompanied of course by Levin. "What are you doing here?"

"We just wanted to make sure you were all right," replied Kitty; "you left in such a hurry . . ."

"By all that is holy under heaven and earth!" Alyosha gasped, staring at Kitty's chest. "Those must be the most glorious breasts *ever!*"

"Shut up, shut up . . ." Vronsky muttered through gritted teeth, slapping covertly at the young man, ". . . I know, but just shut up . . ."

"That was very thoughtful of you," said Anna to Kitty. "But it really wasn't necessary . . ."

"Aw, shit!" swore Oblonsky, thoroughly disgusted. He stood by the table, holding an empty bottle. "Vronsky, you're out of vodka . . ."

"Mr. Oblonsky," Levin retorted hotly, yet with thoroughly disciplined restraint, "I'll thank you to not use such vulgarities with ladies present! I really expected more from a man of your station . . ."

"Vronsky!" The cry came from the doorway, and all turned to see who it was.

"Sonia?!" Vronsky returned, beginning to feel dazed—both physically and mentally—even as the prostitute threw herself into his arms and kissed him deep and hard in a manner only a woman of ill-repute can . . .

"Where have you been?" she asked, pouting, when she had unclenched her lips from his. "You haven't come to visit in so very long . . ."

"Who the hell is she?!?" Anna, Tess, and Lolita demanded in unison.

"Um . . ." Vronsky replied, trying unsuccessfully to free himself from the dexterous and seemingly all-encompassing limbs of his former whore. He was saved—in a manner of speaking—for the moment from answering, as Karenin stepped into the room.

"So here you are!" he accused, standing before Anna red-faced and agitated like a great and angry zit that has gone overlong without popping. "I—your own husband—learn you've returned to Moscow, and where do I hear it from? The wagging tongues of idle wives on the street corner! And then, to add injury to insult, where do I find you, but here—with *him*! And all this rabble, doing God knows what!"

Anna tried to reply, but the words escaped her . . .

"I have just one question for you then," Karenin went on heatedly, yet now also seeming to bristle with discomfort at what he was about to ask; "and I expect you to answer truly—do you love this man?"

Anna looked from Vronsky to her husband, and then back again. "I—"

"Well, well, well, well, well!" roared the deep and sonorous voice of Chimi-khan. "What a busy little throng you've got mustered here!"

"*Chimi-khan?!*" cried Vronsky, utter disbelief taking hold of his being, and ringing away at him as if he were an old, wet sock.

"The one and only!" Chimi-khan replied. "Mongol emperor, Tatar tyrant, Crimean conqueror! In person!"

"What the hell are you doing here?!"

"Chimi-wimi?" Lolita said, stepping forward. "I told you not to follow me . . ."

The mighty warrior blushed and seemed to sink down into himself with embarrassment. "Well, I know . . . but, I mean . . . I couldn't help it, Loly-poo . . ."

"I don't believe it . . ." Vronsky commented, veins bulging out of his forehead. "But I have to believe it, don't I? Because I'm here, and here it all is, and—"

Schopenhauer stood, beginning, "And we are *all*—"

"*SHUT UP!!*" Vronsky bellowed, his face a deep, unhealthy sort of purplish hue. His outburst momentarily quieted the room, but only for a few seconds before everyone returned to whatever they had been doing.

"*Ja* . . ." Schopenhauer muttered, dropping back onto his chair.

"I guess this is about it then," Vronsky laughed, nearing hysterics. "This is everything . . . everything, that is, but for the—"

Just then, Evdokia and the landlady Lizaveta Proknokovnia walked in toting a kitchen sink between them. "Cousin Vronsky!" Evdokia declared, smiling unabashedly.

In response, Vronsky completely lost it . . .

"*Aaaaarrrghhh!!*" he screamed over the din filling his apartment, tearing at his hair and jumping up and down, feeling as if he were being ripped to pieces by the chaos going on all around him. "*What else?! What else can happen!?. . .*"

Chapter Thirteen

As can be seen in the rantings of the generally overlooked Fifteenth Century philosopher Chartreuse who is perhaps best known for having said, "*Bonjoir*, Pierre!" (to no one in particular)—the world is rarely governed by any sort of standard of absolutes; that is to say, reality hardly ever adheres itself to any strict division of, as it were, black and white, but rather is generally reflected as a sort of incandescent yellowish-green that really just sits off to the side over there a bit and tries to be unobtrusive. Initially no one understood what exactly he meant by his theory, but when he elaborated by stating, "Well, take me for example . . ." there were those who began to feel the gist of it.

Never in all the history of philosophical thought—neither Western nor Eastern—had there ever been anything resembling even the tiniest, most remote sort of proof that Chartreuse's Theory of the Inconstancy of Unabsolute Discoloration might be true . . . but as Vronsky tore away at his hair and his clothes and bounced himself bodily about the room, struggling with the ever lessening spark of lucidity that kept total insanity at bay, a thought passed fleetly through his mind: "What if *I* am the doppelganger and it is the real Vronsky who has vanished?!". . . and, though he knew deep down inside himself that he was, indeed, the true Vronsky, his momentary doubt—so soon after the destruction of his double, with the last fading wisps of the doppelganger's essence still clinging to the air in the room—at that precise instant, Chartreuse's theory was proven to be true . . .

Just outside the door to Vronsky's apartment, a dark and fetid mist began to coalesce, tiny sparks of luminous yellow and green twinkling within the growing, smoky mass. A low rumbling grumble began to emit from the forming creature—still a swirling mass of vapors, yet rapidly taking the shape of a man—and the sparks of yellow and green came faster and burned brighter, now accompanied by a dull, darkened red of infernal corruption glowing at its center. It was the creation of the doppelganger's doppelganger—or, as the beast preferred to be called, Vronsky Vronsky Vronsky Vronsky Vronsky Vronsky Vronsky Vronsky . . .

Fortunately for all—and especially for Vronsky himself—the fundamental nature of the demon was almost completely unstable; in being the double of a double, the flaws and imperfections that exist in any creature of physical being were cubed, and thus, before it had even finished birthing itself from the primeval essence of existence itself, the doppelganger's doppelganger imploded into nothingness, leaving in its wake but a lingering stench of sulfur and burnt offal . . .

Chapter Fourteen

Vronsky felt his ears pop and his vision was filled with thousands of tiny, sparkling yellow and green will-o'-the-wisps. He knew nothing of what had just occurred—or rather *nearly* occurred—in the corridor outside the threshold to his apartment (the entire incident reflecting on him in merely a sort of flatulent sensation that doesn't quite want to let go, instead just building and building until you're sure it's going to rupture—and even that was muted by a great angst that can only be described as an overwhelming psychological dysentery), but what he did know was he seemed to have suddenly recovered his natural state of mind . . .

"All right," he said, immediately taking charge of the situation, "enough is enough! You two—" He motioned to Evdokia and Lizavetta Proknokovnia, "—get that sink out of here!" As they hurried to obey, Vronsky scanned the room, seeking the means to remove all those who were not, at the moment, necessary.

"Lolita, my dear!" continued Vronsky, picking her and her Spanish friend as the next to be ousted. "I am, indeed, deeply wounded to hear the love you once felt for me has faded all away—"

"Well," Lolita commented, speaking quietly so Manuel wouldn't hear; "I don't know if it's faded *all* away . . . I might have time for a quick—"

"No, you haven't . . ." Vronsky interrupted, whisking her and Manuel from the apartment.

"Ah, ha!" Schopenhauer was on his feet again, this time waggling his finger in Chimi-khan's face. "I knew I knew you from someplace, but it is only now that it comes to me! You are not this Mongol conquering person at all!"

"I don't know what you're talking about . . ." Chimi-khan nervously denied the accusation, but unconsciously backed away.

"You and I knew each other many years ago—we attended university together," Schopenhauer went on. "And I think your *real* name . . . is Yamyinsky Yamyangovich!"

"No!!" the mighty khan screeched in despair, wringing his hands like a worrisome old woman. "It's a lie!"

"It is truth!" Schopenhauer insisted. "*Ja* . . . it all comes back to me now—you had no interest in your studies, and so you quit school to travel about Finland as a song and dance man!"

"*Aaaaaaahhh!*" the fallen conqueror screamed, dashing out the door, with Schopenhauer in close pursuit, singing Scandinavian show-tunes.

"Schope?" Oblonsky cried, chasing after the German. "Are we going back to the tavern? Schope! Schope! Wait up!"

"My goodness!" declared Kitty, fraught with disapproval at the spectacle going on around her. "My sister will hear of her husband's behavior—you can be sure of that!"

"Perhaps," Vronsky suggested, "Oblonsky warrants a bit of looking after—I'm sure your sister would appreciate it...and you can always stop by to visit Anna again when you've seen your brother-in-law safely home . . ."

"Mr. Vronsky, that is a capital idea," Kitty agreed and, dragging Levin along behind her, she, too, disappeared out the door.

"Ah, good," Vronsky commented, watching them file out down the hallway. "It seems to be going a bit easier . . ."

"Well, then, Vronsky, my sweet," said Tess, "it looks as if the party's beginning to break up . . ." She started as if to perch up on her toes to kiss Vronsky goodbye, but caught Anna's glare out of the corner of her eye and backed down; instead she merely winked, running her hand over his cheek as she passed by him on her way out the door.

"Finally!" Vronsky exclaimed; "I think that's everyone—" Noticing a writhing bulge under the covers on the bed, he walked over and pulled the blanket back.

"Sonia?" he said, surprised. "And *Alyosha*?!"

"Perhaps we'd better find someplace else . . ." Sonia suggested.

"Perhaps . . ." Vronsky agreed. Then to Alyosha he added, "When you have a religious crisis, you really go all out, don't you?"

Alyosha shrugged, blushing slightly, and hurried after Sonia.

"All right then," Vronsky said, peeking under the bed and behind the curtains; "assuming no one is still hiding anywhere . . . this is how it is to be—"

"Oh, no—" Karenin replied boldly; "I'll tell *you* how it is, *MISter* Vronsky! You, sir, are nothing but a beast! I go out of my way to find employment for you, invite you into my home, help you to set up your life here in Moscow—and how do you repay these gestures? By stealing a man's wife!?! These are not the actions of a man, but the lowly endeavors of a mere animal—that's right, Vronsky, a dumb creature of feral and base intentions! You are nothing more than a savage!" Turning his rage to Anna, he said, "And *you* . . . I suppose I might simply say the same, so very weak-willed as you are, like a strange little puppy who betrays her master because someone else has patted her on the head and called her 'good dog' . . . Anna, you know I've been nothing if not a devoted husband . . ."

"Well, you're half right . . ." muttered Vronsky.

Bristling slightly at the jibe, Karenin went on, "Now, I'll ask of you once more Anna: Do you love this *Vronsky?*"

Throughout his entire tirade, Anna's eyes never left Vronsky—as if she took comfort from his being there, as if his very presence shielded her from the scathing words her husband cast out at the two of them. But now she turned to Karenin, standing brave and defiant, a single tear rolling down her cheek. "I do," she replied. "God help us all, but I do love him . . ."

For the briefest of moments Karenin looked as if he might just crumple in on himself and disappear, but then his rage erupted once more—tenfold over what it had been. "You little whore!" he growled; then, emitting a most uncharacteristic roar, he lunged toward Anna and with a resounding slap that seemed to echo through the room, he knocked her to the floor.

A stunned silence followed—none of them quite believing what had just happened—but it took only seconds for Vronsky to recover his shock, and the silence was shattered as he grabbed Karenin by the jacket and hurled him viciously into the wall. His anger not spent, Vronsky then offered a backhanded blow to the chin, and his adversary slumped to the floor.

"You say *I* am a beast, Karenin?" Vronsky spat, tersely, acting as if it took all his effort to not continue pummeling away at the man lying at his feet. "And yet it is you who attacks a defenseless woman! It is you who neglects her and takes her for granted, driving her to find compassion and companionship and love in the arms of another! It is you who is less than a man! Do you know what you are? You are ridiculous and superfluous and a fool! But more than anything, you're bad fish, Karenin—that's what you are! At first, when it's been eaten, everything seems well enough—the void of hunger is alleviated, peace of mind, all that . . . but before long things begin to go awry, everything seems just slightly askew, and the longer it's in there, the more it feels as if that bad fish were swimming all about, roiling and thrashing, and it sends up sour bubbles of regret and ill-intent that stick in your throat until finally you feel your finned friend—who is of course no friend at all in actuality—coursing up the stream of your esophagus as if to spawn in the ever continuing saga of life . . . but then, instead, it gives up entirely at the final moment, disintegrating into a messy, sloppy splay of regurgitated contempt, all down the front of you!"

"But—" Karenin squeaked meekly, cringing at every word of the verbal barrage.

"*Don't* interrupt!" Vronsky growled, dangerously, leaning over to bestow Karenin with a sharp slap in the nose. "I, on the other hand, am good fish—oh, yes, I see you scoff at that, but it's true . . . good fish, indeed! I am the finest fish a woman might delight in—the taste, the texture, the succulent juices that drip down her chin . . . when I am inside her, the gnaw of hunger has been thoroughly sated, she is warm and happy and safe and suffused with a feeling of utter fulfillment . . ."

"And that's all it is to you!" Karenin accused. "My wife claims to love you, but for you it's nothing more than carnal dalliance?"

Vronsky snorted an unamused half-laugh. "What else is there? What else is love, but an overwhelming mix of loneliness and lust getting the better of you? And so you find someone to alleviate those things, someone who doesn't absolutely bore the snot out of you, so it seems not a completely futile waste when you're waiting for the next time to fire up the old whoo-pee-machine . . ."

Slowly gathering himself to his feet, keeping a wary eye on Vronsky, Karenin walked over to where Anna sat. "Is it true? Anna . . . is this what it has all come to? Am I but . . . bad fish? . . ."

Sobbing, Anna hid her face in her kerchief and nodded her head. In a very soft voice, she replied, "You don't realize how I gag! As if there were a tiny fish bone caught in my throat that simply won't let go . . ."

"And . . . him?" he asked, indicating Vronsky with a bitter, though defeated, toss of his head.

"Oh, it's true! It's true! I'm sorry, but it's all true!" Anna cried, burying her face in her hands again. "Vronsky is fresh lake trout, with asparagus and a fine chardonnay!"

Vronsky sat down beside her and held her in his arms, rocking her back and forth soothingly and softly caressing her hair. When she had recovered herself somewhat, Anna looked up to see they were alone.

"Is he—?"

"Yes, my love," Vronsky said warmly, kissing her forehead. "He's gone."

With a sigh, Anna let herself sink completely into Vronsky's embrace. "So...what do we do now?" she asked.

"Hmm . . ." Vronsky said, mulling over the possibilities in his mind. "Well, we could go 'fishing' . . ."

Chapter Fifteen

Throughout his life, whenever Vronsky Vronsky spent any sort of extended period of time with other human beings, it made him acutely aware of just how bothersome it could be that they were not him. This conflict—of being Vronsky, on the one hand, or of not being Vronsky, on the other—occasionally rose up within him from somewhere in the dark and troubled depths of his innermost psyche, and he would be forced to wrestle with the possibility that it might be better to remove himself entirely from the rest of society, to remain forever alone in self-imposed exile from his fellow man . . . but then, inevitably, he would think of some witty remark in need of sharing or he would get that undeniable tingling sensation in his loins, and his ego would again take control, suffusing his being with a triumphant eminence that loomed dauntingly, with gritted, grinding teeth and knotted, bulging muscles in the neck, thrashing away with clenched fists at anything resembling self-doubt (or common sense) that might yet linger in the immediate vicinity, and he would decide perhaps other people were, after all, acceptable enough, and, thus, could be tolerated, if only in small doses . . .

The exception to this, from the day he met her, seemed to be Anna—but after the chaos greeting their return from abroad had died down, and even following Karenin's announcement that he was granting Anna a divorce, making Vronsky absolutely positive such would prove to be the end of their troubles, his love for her began to wear thin. What Vronsky had not counted on was now in addition to feeling guilt over how their relationship had begun, she also felt a failure because her marriage had ended, and she began to rapidly descend into a deep depression. Not only did she constantly worry over how the rest of Muscovite society would judge her for her circumstances—to the point that she eventually refused to even leave their home—but she began feeling extremely jealous; she was convinced Vronsky no longer loved her, because he continued to go out into the world—seemingly leaving her behind . . . and, in general, he continued being Vronsky.

Given Anna's suspicions regarding Vronsky's behavior when he was out were completely unwarranted—though the letter she had found which he had written to Kitty's breasts didn't help matters any . . . (in his own defense, he had written the letter months earlier, before he and Anna had become intimate)—he possessed very little empathy for her discomfiture. Vronsky had always been of a mind if someone whom he had given no reason to look upon him with mistrust mistrusted him anyway, thereafter he would try to live up to those deluded expectations—thus, if Anna was going to wrongfully accuse him of cheating on her, and nothing he could say or do would convince her otherwise, out of his very love of her (and, in all honesty, a goodly bit of spite added to the mix . . .), he would do what he could to make her not wrong. It wasn't that Vronsky wanted to hurt Anna, but the truth of the matter was he found her much less appealing now—half-maddened by guilt and jealousy and what have you, all pale and sickly and frail from loss of appetite and inaction of being as she was—than when he had first met her, a warm, vibrant, passionate, and neglected wife of another man. And, quite frankly, he was more than a little offended she could so ignominiously lose her grasp on sanity as she had, with little or no regard for his own feelings; at times he could hardly believe her audacity, to just blatantly go mad—and with no consideration toward him, even after he went to all the effort of falling in love with her . . . really, he thought, she should expect to get what she gets . . .

When Tess came looking for him—of course still having no idea the Vronsky she knew had not been, in actuality, the genuine article—he initially had no interest in betraying Anna. Oh, of course he still looked and wished and desired, and Anna's growing mental instability did nothing to ease his course along the road of monogamy, but he had not been with another woman since he and Anna's affair had begun in earnest. Tess, however, proved to be quite persistent and it did not take long before Vronsky was forced to admit the doppelganger's taste in women was most extraordinary— indeed, he soon found her to be thoroughly irresistible, and though he had not, as of yet, had sex with her, he knew it was imminent . . . the only reason such a happenstance had not occurred was due to the excess to which Tess drank—and so, on the two occasions in which Vronsky had already met with her, they would inevitably pass out before anything happened; when he awoke she was gone, having left him money on the bedside table with her usual note of something to the effect of "It was marvelous—as always . . . Love, Tess."

It was as he prepared to leave for a rendezvous with Tess, seeing Anna sitting as she always sat, unmoving and seemingly oblivious in the pain of her own existence, that Vronsky felt a pang of regret. The icy grip of a deep remorse—nearly a sense of mourning—seized his heart momentarily at the vision of this shadow, this shade of the woman she had been . . .

"I was just going out for a while, Anna dear," he said. "I . . . would you like to come along?" he added, feeling an almost hopeful surge of emotion, that was quickly replaced by panic—*what if she said yes?!* What could he tell Tess?! What was he thinking—inviting her on his date?! An image of the three of them together flashed through his mind, and suddenly an intense arousal supplanted the compassion and affection he had been feeling. He shook the image from his head—Anna would never agree to such a thing!—and waited nervously for her answer.

At first it seemed she had not even heard him, and a response would not be forthcoming, but then she looked up from where she stared at nothing.

Her eyes, dull and listless and gray, looked into his, and she forced a wane smile. "No, Vronsky . . . thank you." She sighed and, though she did not look away from him, returned to staring into nothing.

A flood of relief passed through him—and as it did, Vronsky wondered why it failed to make him feel any better. He continued standing there for several moments, simply looking on her—remembering without really remembering, feeling without completely feeling...and then he realized Anna's eyes had regained their focus once more, and it was she who looked upon him. She no longer slumped in her chair, but sat straight, an expression of . . . not quite contentment—perhaps resolve—playing across her features . . . as if she had come to some sort of decision, and in surrendering herself to her fate, she was released from the dark void in which she had been floundering . . .

"Well, then," he said; "if you're sure . . ."

"Yes, I'm quite certain, Vronsky darling," she replied with a calmness and a purposefulness he had never before witnessed in her, and an intensity in her eyes he had not seen since the day they had met, so many months ago at the Moscow station. "There's something I've been meaning to do."

Suddenly feeling very ill at ease, he was anxious to be away; nevertheless he hesitated. "I suppose . . . well, what shall you do then?"

Anna smiled—a determined smile that contained no warmth whatsoever—and replied, "I have a train to catch . . ."

Reading from Tolstoy

Not a god,
not a man . . .
not even
an over-glorified,
over-indulging,
over-zealous,
yet under-achieving
ape—
magnanimously superior
and self-aggrandizing,
picking nits
from his fur
as he squats in
the squishy squalor
of his existence . . .
(—though, probably,
the last rings most true . . .)

"She loves me,
she loves me not . . .
she loves me—"
*"Are you **still** living?!"*
"No—I died long ago . . .
but you already knew,
didn't you . . .
you better than anyone . . ."

The penultimately procrastinated,
born of Epimethial unintent . . .
malingering, stagnating—
'til Destiny arrives,

sweeping into my life
like a warm, spring breeze,
and verily blowing me away!
She takes me bodily
into her naked embrace—
then rejects me—
shuns me!
pariah!!—
leaving us with pasts
each had found unfulfilling . . .
eternity remaining unoffered . . .

Later, she reads to me:
'Then do this for me—
never utter
such words again,
and let us
be good friends . . .'
'Friends we
shall never be.
You know that
Yourself . . .'

Does it even really change anything?
I mean . . . I suppose I've always known
exactly who and what I am—
yet I was completely unprepared
as undeniable reality
smacked me in the face with it . . .

Grains or grasses
or caustic chemicals—
the elixir of beloved,

soul-sustaining,
fermented potato nectar!. . .
drugs and booze and wh—
. . . ritual bleedings . . .
yet nothing can erase
the misdeeds and misdirections,
the myriad of misgivings
that have led to ruin . . .
without her,
nothing can make of me
more than I am,
when it was she
—the predilection of
all my proclivities—
who did ever inspire me
unto all I might be . . .

She reads:
'I am lost, lost!
Worse than lost!
I'm like an
over-strained
violin string
that must snap . . .'

All I ever wanted
was to be real . . .
I know now
such can never be.

Ludmila of Tverskaya Street
(a play in three acts)

dramatis personae:

Igor – a hopeless romantic

Ludmila – his (hopefully) requited love

ACT I – SCENE 1
[A shipyard. IGOR enters.]

IGOR: "Damn, damn, damn, damn, damn! *DAMN!!* Why are all the women going to Tuscany to lose their virtue!? Oh—of course!—there is the culture and the weather and the scenery . . . and, I suppose, if that's your thing, there are those who might sneak from these unwholesomely hole-some women said virtue . . . swarthy, smarmy, swarming unkempt creatures, beasts with bulging eyes and insipidness over-flowing and—

"Alas! I am submerged in the gloppy, burbling gravy of penumbral disillusionment . . . how the hell did that happen?! Well, whoopee-fuck then . . . Idyllic interruptus—what else is new . . ."

[LUDMILA enters, dressed to the hilt—red dress, black nylons, high heels, black nail polish and lip-stick.]

IGOR: "What ho! Lookie-lookie! The magic of her form casts the spell of its function over my waiting whiles—a parasitic pre-dalliance in the offering . . . I feel overwhelmed with the paradox of passion versus preeminence. Forsooth—I must know this woman!

"Milady! Alack—forgive my boldness . . ."

LUDMILA: *[Warily, considering his worth.]* "You are forgiven."

IGOR: "I would know you, if you would . . .?"

LUDMILA: "I would not!"

IGOR: "But your transcending beauty—I cannot contain myself! My love explodes from the very center of my soulful sphere, as if an holistic goiter popped and splaying greedily!"

LUDMILA: "Stop! Say no more! I shall hear no more of this!"

IGOR: "But—"

LUDMILA: "Very well...you may follow me for a time—but only if you promise to never again speak of such things . . ."

IGOR: "Oh, happy day! I am yours!"

LUDMILA: "Hmm...yes, well, we shall see . . ."

[Exeunt.

ACT I – SCENE 2
[A hayloft. LUDMILA is lounging in the hay as IGOR enters.]

IGOR: "Tut-tut, Ludmila! What a beautiful day, and here I find you lofting about in the hay! Why are you so sad?"

LUDMILA: "Nothing's right . . . nothing matters . . ."

IGOR: "But you matter—to me, anyway—and I like to believe that I matter to you . . . in some way. We should do something—we should run away!"

LUDMILA: "If only we could . . . someplace far from here . . ."

IGOR: "Where? Sandy beaches? Lush, green forests? Dangerous, rocky precipices? Where would you like to go?"

LUDMILA: "I don't know . . . wherever you want—whatever makes you happy . . ."

IGOR: "But don't you know? Only you can do that . . ."

LUDMILA: "I'll bet you'd say love should always come before money, before all else."

IGOR: "There have been times in my life when I've felt I loved a woman enough that we could have had a 'happily-ever-after'—it was the rest of the world that got in the way. . ."

LUDMILA: "Am I one of those women? Because—well, I mean . . . I've just always thought that we would be so good together—if things were different, I mean . . . we think so much alike, we feel the same about so many things, believe in the same things . . . I just . . . I don't know—but what a great couple we would make, don't you think? The way we always connect so well and have such a wonderful time together, and—but, well—no, nevermind . . . I don't want to know."

IGOR: ". . . thanks . . ."

LUDMILA: "Better luck next life."
[Exeunt.

153

ACT I – SCENE 3

[The summit of Mount Kilimanjaro. LUDMILA and IGOR enter.]

IGOR: "It's amazing, isn't it?"

LUDMILA: "What is?"

IGOR: "I've never felt so high!"

LUDMILA: "The higher the better . . ."

IGOR: "And it isn't merely the altitude, you know—I . . . well, perhaps I shouldn't say . . . oh, but I must! I could kiss you!

"But what have I said?! Forgive me, Ludmila! I beg you! I apologize with all the profusity at my mustering! Besides, I was only kidding, of course!" *[Forced, and unconvincing laughter.]* "However, I do apologize, for this is no place for fooling around . . . well, I mean—you know . . . unless *you* want to fool around . . . but I'm not going to hand you a load of crap here . . . well, I mean—unless you *want* . . . well, I suppose, neither literally nor figuratively shall I bestow unto you any quantity of feces!—for, truly, whatever my intentions, such could but act to besmirch and soil your immaculate personage in just a really stinky sort of way, and—

"Oh! Caution be damned! I can refrain no longer—looking out, as we are, from the very top of the world...doesn't it all just seem so . . . so insignificant?! I promised to be only your friend, but, my Ludmila, I love you! I love you! I love you!"

LUDMILA: "I love you, too!"

IGOR: "You do? Why did you never say?"

LUDMILA: "I only just realized—though now I think I must have loved you all along! . . . Igor—my darling!"

IGOR: "Oh, Ludmila! My sweetie-pants!"

LUDMILA: "You may kiss me now, if you'd like . . ." *[IGOR passionately kisses her.]* "You're perfect!"

IGOR: "Ah—nothing is perfect, my love . . . though you come very close—and I have a pretty nice butt!"

LUDMILA: "Oh, and yet—woe is we! We find ourselves at the summit of a grand and majestic mountain . . . I fear there is no place left for us to venture but downward . . ."

IGOR: "Then we shall take wing and soar through the endless heavens!"

LUDMILA: "I don't know if I can . . . I have forgotten how to fly."

IGOR: "Then I will hold you—and our love will take us aloft! For all of time, Ludmila, I will hold you, and we shall be borne on the wings of our love beyond the boundaries of the cosmos!. . ." *[They kiss.]*

[Exeunt.

ACT II – SCENE 1
[The Black Forest. IGOR enters.]

IGOR: "My desire swells within—to touch her and kiss her, to caress and hold and taste her in her nakedly consummate all-overness. She obsesses me—and not just my mind, either, I'll have you know, for I find other parts of me thinking of her quite a little bit as well . . ."

[LUDMILA enters.]

IGOR: "My sweetness! My flower! My sparkling ray of sunshine through the rain!" [They kiss.]

LUDMILA: "Hello, my darling! I'm sorry I'm late…but I had a stone in my shoe, and I had to stop to take it out . . ."

IGOR: "Your poor, dainty, little foot! I—oh! I am crazy!"

LUDMILA: "And I am crazy, too!"

IGOR: "I can't go on!"

LUDMILA: "Oh—do! Do!"

IGOR: "Your feet! I am obsessed with the thought of your feet! I have never seen them—and I long to know them, as I long to know every inch of your brilliant loveliness! How the thoughts of holding your feet consumes me! To know their caress—and to massage them and kiss them and lick them and suck upon their pulchritudinous digits . . . I must make love to your feet, Ludmila!"

LUDMILA: "Oh, my! Really?!"

IGOR: "But, I mean . . . well . . . you know—like only a little bit . . . not to *completion* or anything—just as a stop along the way of the total journey of making love to your all-over . . . I wouldn't want you to think I was weird or anything . . ."

LUDMILA: "This is a new blouse—do you like it?"

IGOR: "I love it! I've never before seen a blouse so blue!"

LUDMILA: "I think it makes my breasts look proud."

IGOR: "They are proud—and I am proud of them as well! You know, your breasts really are quite perfect . . ."

LUDMILA: "Don't tease me!"

IGOR: "Oh, but, my love, I am not—they are as perfect as the rest of your supple form. I have always preferred more modest breasts—I find otherwise to be udderly unbecoming! At times, your breasts seem shy, nearly reclusive, and before their perfection might be known, one would have to coax them out of hiding with promises of love and compassion and happiness—and naughty things all about! But, beset as they are now by your beautiful blouse of blue, your breasts beckon to me—calling out a bold greeting of good will and fortunate tidings, as if a long-known, bosom friend, just returning from an extended holiday abroad, bearing gifts!"

LUDMILA: "I love you!"

IGOR: "I love *you*!!"

LUDMILA: "Come—I'll put my bra on my feet and dance around for you, and then you can fan me with palm fronds and feed me grapes! . . ."

[Exeunt.

ACT II – SCENE 2
[A grocery story. IGOR and LUDMILA enter.]

IGOR: "I don't like it here . . ."

LUDMILA: "Why not?"

IGOR: "I don't know . . . there's just something about it all—the way it's arranged maybe, with just everything all over in haphazard fashion . . . it makes me . . . uneasy . . . "

LUDMILA: "Well, I promise, darling, we'll never have to come to this grocery store again."

IGOR: "What?! How can you say that? Devil-woman! How you, at times, do torment me with your taunting wiles! But I love you! I do—you know I do! It's not on purpose, I understand that, but can't you see, the only reason I can stand it at all is because *you're* here . . . having you with me is the only thing that keeps me going—you are my sole strength, and safely hidden away from the woes of the world as we are, behind this indomitable aegis of our conjoining love, there is no heavenly height of transcendence to which we might not aspire! Never come here again?—I don't think so. Indeed, we should come back on this very day each year, just to say, *Dammit all to hell! We are here, and we are together, ready to stand firm in the face of adversity, invincible in the sanctimonious embrace of our loving union!*"

LUDMILA: "Whatever . . ."

IGOR: "I love you, dearest, darling Ludmila!!"

LUDMILA: "Here—have a cookie . . ."

[Exeunt.

ACT II – SCENE 3
[A cemetery. IGOR enters.]

IGOR: "In darkening shades of night—I await the bedazzlement of my love's beauty!"

[LUDMILA enters and embraces IGOR.]

LUDMILA: "My darling—how I've missed you!"

IGOR: "And I you!"

LUDMILA: "But why did we have to meet here, surrounded by death?"

IGOR: "For the peace and serenity of each's other uninterrupted—surrounded by, yet untouchable to, death, safe with the life of our conjoined love surging through us!"

LUDMILA: "You're sweet . . . I'm surging, too!" *[Kisses him.]*

IGOR: "Oh, my beloved Ludmila—how your lips inspire me! I long to lionize you with poetry, expressing all that you mean to me!

"Oh! I've just had a notion! Let me write a poem across your being! Let me strip these clothes from your beauteous body and cover you, from your head to your tantalizing, little toes, spiraling down and around your splendorous form—a bold declaration of my overwhelming love, affection, and desire for you, my goddess!"

LUDMILA: "You're so silly!"

IGOR: "But I am entirely serious! You shall be the parchment of my soul—and I shall come to you and bask in your naked splendor . . . while my pen is held erect and ready to begin it's loving, adoring task across the very slate of your inspiration!"

LUDMILA: "You're beautiful!"

IGOR: "No—*you're* beautiful! My love for you shall burn for all of time!"

LUDMILA: "And I . . . well—that is . . . I mean . . ."

IGOR: "My darling! What's the matter?! What is this malaisial fog that seeps over you?"

LUDMILA: "I've just realized—I don't love you anymore."

IGOR: "But—how can this be?!"

LUDMILA: "In fact, I'm not sure I ever loved you . . ."

IGOR: "No!"

LUDMILA: "Sorry for the confusion."   *[Exits.*

IGOR: "*Ludmila!!*"

[Exeunt.

ACT III – SCENE 1
[The gates of Hell. IGOR enters.]

IGOR: *[Soliloquizing.]* "So what hath love wrought for me? What, now, hath love taught to me? . . . Never to be honest, never sincere—always hold something back, and skew the truth to serve mine own purposes . . . for her mind is forever her own, and e'en that which she may profess to share will be amok with her own thwarting misdirections. Never to have expectations— act, if you must, but expect nothing in return . . . the heart is but an organ to pump blood and prolong one's existence . . . open it in earnest to another and it is but a matter of time ere it is expunged from your person—which is fine if you can then just fall down and die, but, in truth, by god, you can yet exist in pained torment with a vacuous, raw, bleeding cavity where said organ once lay. Appeal, instead, only to her cunt—the true seat of her emotions— for that she may open to you, but her heart she never will. If ever it seems you have within your grasp whatever *Everything* you think may fulfill you, that at last the world seems to make sense—turn and run the other way, never look back . . . for it is but an illusion, nothing more, and if it dissipates while it holds you in its nimbus of deceptions, your soul will fade with it. Remain forever alone . . . for the rigors of the solitary life may cause you to waste ever away—still better by far than to submit one's existence to the violent doom and living death of another's love. . .

"Oh, and—perhaps—I should eat more soups . . ."

[A little, wing'd MONKEY-MAN on a tricycle and a GREEK CHORUS enter.]

GREEK CHORUS: *[Singing, as they stone IGOR.]* "Etcetera! Etcetera! Etcetera!~"

MONKEY-MAN: "Bananas!"

[Death.

finis .

Big Julie's Radish Entourage
. . . of Bloody Rot Snot Yuck (Uh!) and the Heinousness of Living in a World of Eternal Ambiguity and Ambivalent Angst (Part I Mayakovsky's Ghost, and How It Engorged Potemkin's Spleen)

It was a day in which
nothing would happen . . .
and I was ready!
—the dog days of summer,
and I was steppin' in it . . . . . .

*(lethargy of living in
the itching of my spleen)*

—saw a guy who
looked like Mayakovsky
(only living)—just walking
down the street with
his lovely Lily leading along
to his ill-fated loaded gun . . .
ah, mine own beloved Dzivagura!
—*O poshlaya devitsa!*—
I don't know where you are . . .

*(one never knows . . .well,
alright—one <u>sometimes</u> knows . . .
or (at least) might wonder)*

—and then there's
the little kitty in the window,
and it started barking at me—
and now my knee hurts . . .

(Satan is upon us!!)
—all uphill from here . . .
by evening—this I know—
'twill be, yet again, but
the veritable groundhogsday
of fetid, potemkinish umbrage . . .

—one week in July . . .
(infinite visions of chaos
dragged down by heavy heart,
obscured thought in delusions
of soulful disjunction)
—and then there is death.

The 13th Apostle

. . . inspired by V. Mayakovsky's 'A Cloud in Trousers'
[translated by Andrey Kneller]

The night oozed through the room and sank. The burden of it lay heavily upon my heart . . . the long hours waiting for her—four o'clock, she'd said, not arriving 'til the stroke of midnight. Yet there was a momentary spark within—there had been nothing, only the night, emptiness in the dark, and then she appeared! But the spark faded, replaced again by the nervous aggravation I had felt all those hours waiting, with the first glance into eyes that once held me warmly in their embrace, and now shielded me, held me at bay . . . lips from which I had known such passionate kisses, from which I had known such wonder and bliss by the caress of loving words, singing the song of her soul—now tersely clenched, unwilling to reveal her purpose . . .

Her eyes fell to where she was wringing away at her gloves—her anxiousness a palpable presence between us . . . I didn't honestly know if the silent stasis looming would momentarily drive me mad, or if I preferred to stay in that moment forever—just to be here with her, away from the world without . . . but, exasperated, she reasserted herself to her intention.

"You know," she began, gazing determinedly into my eyes—as if to calm a wild beast, "I'm getting married soon . . ."

And all the tension drained away; in its place a moment of utter inner oblivion . . . "Oh, yes...*that* . . ." I spoke with a casual bravado that but a moment earlier—and a moment hence—would have been a lie. "Of course, thereafter . . . we'll have to be . . . discrete . . ."

I had hoped for a smile—a roll of her eyes, anything! Was the mockery I suddenly felt in her expression, in her bearing—or was it in my heart? My life was passing before me in a blur, and all of it felt through her . . . still I am sure I seemed perfectly calm . . . which, I am told, can be more terrifying than when I let go the rage . . . this was confirmed to me when she, as if involuntarily, by the very force of my emotion, took a step back—the condescending pity I sensed a moment earlier now replaced by a preternatural survival instinct . . . her task accomplished, she wanted nothing more than to flee . . .

The rest was a chaotic nebula of sanguinary bile, and red and black shimmerings of an inner tempest, and the acrid undoing of despair . . . no longer a man—something set aside from humanity . . . as if a cloud in trousers . . . in the unmindful mental morass of love's foggy bottom blues . . . *(butanyhoo . . .)*

When she had gone *(—had the screaming of her name after her been real, or part of the inner nightmare? (Did it matter!?)—)*, in my teeth, again, I held the hardened crust of last night's caresses . . . the world spinning wildly out of control!—exploding all around!—fading into oblivion!—plummeting into the abyss!—

A shot peals out—

"Drink Cocoa—Van Houten!"

The rest . . . is silence.

finis.

The Road from Taganrog

The gods pour scorn down upon me:
"Thy belligerence, O Zakharin,
doth, indeed, run amok!"

"An so say I to ye—
blow it out yer collective, deified ass! . . .
(—not that I at all disagree . . .)"

"Thou dare'st to taunt death
with such brazen disregard?!
Thou wouldst deign to mock eternity
an the predilections of thine intended dissolution!?"

"And, yet, is not death itself eternity?—
antithesis to life's transience . . .
methinks thine indignation doth be misplaced . . ."

"Listen, here, thou smarmy, little fu—"

—Curmudgeon gods be damned!
Enough of death and life—
of eternity, infinity, relativity, proximity . . .
a proclivity toward inanity—
an ere a chimeara'd tranquility gives way
unto the penultimate crappicity of reality . . . . . .

The inculcations of mine inebriations
do but invoke an unctuous innocuousness . . .
the incrementation—
of my **spleen!** . . .

"Oh, help me, Irene!!"
(—I don't know what I mean . . .)

Tumultuous antagonisms
of prodigious entanglements
—harangue . . .
protean prophet or superfluous man—
liberal idealism or rational egoism . . .
the quintessential question:
Who will I be?
*(When?-Where?-What?-How?-**Why!?!**)*

. . . in the darkness—dying . . .
wallowing in the wake
of the wiles of the world . . .
or in the bright light of being—
belying the darkness dwelling within . . .
a capitulation to the viability of hope—
that might never become the actuality
of that long sought-after fruition . . . . . .

Le Morte de Vronsky

dramatis personae:

Raskolnikov – a naïve, young Russian man

Vronsky – a voice in Raskolnikov's head; Siberian 'prophet' of the mad god
Xalmoxis

Potemkin – another voice in Raskolnikov's head; Cossack demon minion of
the goddess Kali

Groznyi – a voice in Potemkin's head

Nadia – a maiden fair

Mosiaga Nuninovich – an acquaintance of Raskolnikov

6 muzhiks (Russian peasants)

Scene 1

_[A moonlit night in a lush, green garden; silvery-blue lighting; NADIA enters
to balcony overlooking gardens below. Whene'er VRONSKY speaks,
NADIA's lighting dims.]_

NADIA: "O brazen moon, to look down upon me so! Thy silence echoes
within my soul, to nearly deafen me—where shall mine heart lay?" _[Sighs.]_
"Though many have tried to claim it, who shall possess this gilded prize of
my love which pulses out mine yearnings here within my breast? Who shall
hold me as his own 'til Death's jealous embrace doth claim me for his eternal
desire? Alas! Forsooth . . . 'tis by the silver splendor o' Luna's glowing
visage that my musings wander toward madness . . . love, death, madness—
madness, love, an' death—how it all doth make mine head ache!"

[Enter RASKOLNIKOV (and VRONSKY in his head) below.]

RASKOLNIKOV: "But soft! What light 'pon yonder window breaks?"

VRONSKY: <'Tis the moonlight's reflection cast down from the window's pane—O how I feel its 'pain' to be so transparent to an image so brilliantly beautiful!—yet, Raskolnikov, my comrade, *mien freund*, mine overly hirsute little buddy, look to the girl . . . for she, methinks, doth seem quite the hotty-vixen-babe, that one!>

RASKOLNIKOV: *[Aside, to VRONSKY.]* "'Twas the woman of which I spoke, vile spirit whoso wiles at mine will with his witless 'what-have-you'! By my troth, she is a vision from heaven—an angel, pure! A goddess, divine!"

VRONSKY: <A demoness, desirous, if thou doth have any luck at all . . .>

RASKOLNIKOV: *[To VRONSKY.]* "Nay, 'tis not lust wherefore I am moved—but by love! Love o' deepest virtue an' purity an'—"

VRONSKY: <Aye, aye—an' blah, blah, blah . . . then thou art Fortune's Fool! For 'tis not the wise man who shall guide his actions upon the deceptions created by mere visions.>

RASKOLNIKOV: "And yet not mere visions—but revelations from on high, epiphanies from heaven sent—"

NADIA: "Alack! A voice from out the darkness—surely the madness doth be upon me! O luminous Selene, in the radiance o' thine wisdom hath thou no mercy 'pon thy humble, devoted priestess?!"

VRONSKY: <Bah! 'Tis as any other of her addle-brained species—thinking a sound in the night to be the mischief o' the full moon . . . aye, if such doth be her pleasure, I say, shouldst we act as the lycanthrope?—to

pounce down upon her maidenhead, howl in victory at said same moon, and, if such be Destiny's decree, put her with pups? . . .>

RASKOLNIKOV: *[To VRONSKY.]* "Nay! Stay thy prurient endeavor, Vronsky, thou vulgar fiend! She doth be not for the likes o' thee!"

VRONSKY: <By almighty Xalmoxis, great deity whom I serve—I do hereby forswear . . . e'en as some hath deemed my lord mad, methinks this loony lass would be greatly pleasing to carry his issue forth unto the world . . .>

RASKOLNIKOV: "I care not what thy mad god desires! I'll not be your instrument—ere I have will to call mine own, she shall not be his!"

VRONSKY: <Well, then, mine other self . . . if thou wouldst have her, make thy play . . . >

NADIA: "Who goes now in the lushness of my garden this night? Speak, if thou be not spirit nor delusion!"

RASKOLNIKOV: "Milady! Fear not, for I am neither . . ."

NADIA: "Then what sort of creature art thou, O spectre in the night?"

RASKOLNIKOV: "I . . . I . . ."

VRONSKY: <Ay-yi-yi-yi-yi!>

RASKOLNIKOV: *[To Vronsky.]* "Thou art right—I am a fool! If only I knew how to pick up women!"

VRONSKY: <Lift wi' the legs . . .>

RASKOLNIKOV: *[To VRONSKY.]* "Mine heart doth fly 'pon eagles wings, yet my mind doth sink as lead to the ocean's floor; my tongue lolls as a floundering carp upon the shore, though I would have it flutter an' soar through buoyant bursts of air upon the wind! Help me, Vronsky—my friend, my brother!—help me, thou who art ne'er without words of wisdom with which to woo! . . ."

VRONSKY: <Egads! Huzzah, I say—huzzah, indeed, huzzah! How quickly hath I evolved from 'vulgar fiend' to belov'd 'brother', methinks, upon thy dreary needs or wants!>

NADIA: "Hello? Art thou yet there?"

RASKOLNIKOV: "Aye, I'll be wi' thee in a moment, milady . . ." *[To VRONSKY.]* "Doth not thou oft' profess to 'Vronsky for Vronsky's sake'? Well, 'tis a moment o' 'Raskolnikov for Raskolnikov's sake'!"

VRONSKY: *[Snorts derisively.]* <That's a mouthful . . . yet I see not what such hast to do with me . . .>

RASKOLNIKOV: *[To VRONSKY.]* "Thou doth dwell within my person—if mine intentions o' love persevere an' succeed, thou would benefit as much as I by the outcome . . ."

VRONSKY: <Hmm . . .well, there doth be that—a front row seat, so to speak . . .though in leaving the matter entirely to me, 'twould be quicker in the coming *(as it were . . .).*>

RASKOLNIKOV: *[To VRONSKY.]* "No doubt . . . an' yet, methinks, 'twill work best for both to work together—the richly ore'd vein o' thy silver-tipped tongue, tempered by the forge o' my compassion an' common sense . . ."

VRONSKY: <Aye, yea, aye—I see thy point . . . very well, then—let me see . . . tell her thou art a pilgrim who hath journeyed far . . .>

RASKOLNIKOV: "Milady!"

NADIA: "Oh, art thou yet here? 'Tis rude to have a lady wait on thee so . . ."

RASKOLNIKOV: "By thy brilliant beauty blinded, I could seek not the words I would say unto thee 'til mine inner sight had been restored!"

NADIA: "Thou doth express thyself well, stranger . . . methinks I shall forgive thee—though only if thou wilt answer mine inquiry . . . what manner o' man or beast doth thou be?"

VRONSKY: <A pilgrim . . .>

RASKOLNIKOV: "O maiden most fair—I doth be but an humble pilgrim who hath traveled far!"

NADIA: "A pilgrim? Art thou, then, a monk? What seeks a *holy* man in my garden by night?!"

VRONSKY: <Well, seeking a 'hole', o' course . . .>

RASKOLNIKOV: "Oh—uh . . . not that sort o' pilgrim . . . *(methinks . . .)*"

VRONSKY: <Tell her thou art a pilgrim who would worship before the altar of her pulchritudinous ambient . . .>

RASKOLNIKOV: "I am a pilgrim who would worship—" *[To VRONSKY.]* "What doth the rest o' that mean, precisely?"

VRONSKY: <In essence, that she doth be really quite hot . . .>

RASKOLNIKOV: "—who would worship…at the shrine o' thy celestially inspiring loveliness!"

NADIA: *[Gasping—but in a good way . . .]* "Truly, then, thou art no monk!"

VRONSKY: <Or, at any rate, not a very good one . . .>

RASKOLNIKOV: "Nay, not a monk—but a big, naughty monkey, swinging through the jungle in search o' the perfect banana!"

VRONSKY: <Oh, brother! Who said thou couldst improvise?!>

NADIA: *[Laughing.]* "And am I the banana thou doth seek?"

RASKOLNIKOV: "In truth, I knew not that which I sought—'til I beheld thee . . . and now, needs must I admit, thou art, as the proverbial banana doth go, really quite 'appealing'!"

NADIA: "Thou art most gracious, good pilgrim!"

VRONSKY: <Holy crud—I canst believe not 'tis working! Why, again, doth I be here?>

NADIA: "Pray, step out from the shadows so I might see thee by Luna's light . . ."

RASKOLNIKOV: *[To VRONSKY.]* "O grievous woe and angst! Would that I had shaved this morning! What if she cares not for the haphazard appearance of her would-be suitor? What if she takes me for a heinous *skank!* and bestrews down upon me with harsh words an' refuse? What if she scorns me, finding mine image most ungentle, an' calls for aid by her father or—alas—the local constable?!"

VRONSKY: <Mayhap thou shouldst hath thought all that ere thou didst go traipsing through her garden in the middle o' the night . . .>

RASKOLNIKOV: *[To VRONSKY.]* "Bah! 'Tis no time for logic—this doth be a matter o' love, an' making sense doth take no part in it!"

VRONSKY: <Well, as logic might be done without—and, o' that, who am I to say it nay?—if 'what-ifs' doth be thy concern, then *what if* thou shouldst step out to be seen and worry o'er the consequences whence they hadst been presented and not merely postulated?>

RASKOLNIKOV: *[To VRONSKY.]* "There doth be a certain clarity of vision by thine words—an' to be enacted in my noble endeavors, I agree! She seemed warmed by the beatitudes of my banter—the spark of her affections hath already been lit! What fear shouldst I to proceed!" *[To NADIA, stepping from the shadows.]* "Milady!"

NADIA: *[Aside.]* "Finally . . ." *[To RASKOLNIKOV.]* "Milord!"

VRONSKY: <Although . . .>

RASKOLNIKOV: *[To VRONSKY, shuffling back into the shadows.]* "Uh! Fiend! Now what says thou?!"

VRONSKY: <Well . . . I was just thinking . . . thou doth want her not to think that thou art . . . uptight. Right?>

RASKOLNIKOV: *[To VRONSKY.]* "Heavens, no! I want her to know my heart is free! That my mind soars to discover all that doth yet be unknown! That my very soul, an if the air itself, rises in surging gusts of passionate love and adoration unto the supernal heights in which I hath found her boundless beauty!"

VRONSKY: <Well . . . I kind of wonder where the hell all that was when thou wert going on about bananas . . . but such doth be neither, nither, nor nyet! Methinks to show her thy spirit doth be, by troth, so free, mayhap . . .>

RASKOLNIKOV: *[To VRONSKY.]* "Yes?! What, what!?"

VRONSKY: <Slip thy pants off.>

RASKOLNIKOV: *[To VRONSKY.]* "No, I . . . *really?!*"

VRONSKY: <Oh, aye, yea—chicks dig that! Such doth allow for them to see the full package straight from the start . . . it shows not merely a free spirit, but an uncommon confidence—and a brazen integrity . . .>

RASKOLNIKOV: *[To VRONSKY.]* ". . . All right! 'Twill be done! Huzzah!!" *[To NADIA, slipping off his pants.]* "Milady!—ready or not, here doth comes me! . . . . . ."

[Fade to black.]

Scene 2
[A bustling city square; gray, drab lighting; RASKOLNIKOV and MOSIAGA enter from opposite directions. 'Extras' wander in and out through the scene, including the 6 MUZHIKs.]

MOSIAGA: "Raskolnikov! It has been ages! What say you?"

RASKOLNIKOV: "Mosiaga—my friend! We are well met—and, yet, I am filled with dire woe!"

MOSIAGA: "No! Woe?!"

RASKOLNIKOV: "Aye, woe! Such dire and heinous, hurtful woe!"

MOSIAGA: "Ah, yes . . . dire, heinous and hurtful…that's the worst kind to have . . ."

RASKOLNIKOV: "Tell me why!?—why does God punish me so?!"

MOSIAGA: "The First Noble Truth tells us that all life is suffering . . ."

RASKOLNIKOV: "Then that explains it—for I have two lives . . . thus I must suffer twice the woe!"

MOSIAGA: "*Two* lives?! My friend, explain yourself! Are you sick? Do you have a disease?"

RASKOLNIKOV: "A disease! Yes, yes though I, myself, am the disease! I am sick of heart—and, most assuredly, sick of mind!"

MOSIAGA: "Oh, assuredly! Assuredly! You're clearly out of your freakin' gourd, my comrade!"

RASKOLNIKOV: "Thank you…you're so soothing to my troubled heart . . ."

MOSIAGA: "Yes, your heart—again with your heart . . . troubled and sick . . ."

RASKOLNIKOV: "Aye, my friend, such is the source of my woe—the disease I carry is here within me . . . deep in my chest, beating ever away, pumping the taint of life's blood throughout my physicality to pollute the very central sphere of being!" *[Whispering.]* "And, also—I have been possessed by some infernal spirit!!"

MOSIAGA: "Okay, all right, all right, okay—now, now, just one thing at a time here . . . you say you have a disease of the heart? Well, that's no problem whatsoever! They now have a cure for that!"

MUZHIK #1: "Pardon me, but I couldn't help but hear . . . they have a cure for what?"

MOSIAGA: "Heart disease!"

MUZHIK #1: "And there's a cure!? Astounding! I had no idea!"

MUZHIK #2: "No idea about what?"

MUZHIK #1: "This man has a disease—but it can be cured!"

MUZHIK #2: "Praise the Virgin! Who would have thought it?"

MUZHIK #3: "Who would have thought what?"

MUZHIK #2: "This man's disease . . . they have a cure!"

MUZHIK #3: "It is a miracle! Why have we not heard of this before?"

MUZHIK #4: "What haven't you heard?"

MUZHIK #3: "There is a cure for this man's disease!"

MUZHIK #4: "A cure?! The Tsar be praised!"

MUZHIK #3: "But there no longer is a Tsar . . ."

MUZHIK #4: "Then praise the Empress Maria (in exile) instead!"

MUZHIK #5: "Huzzah!! The Empress Maria (in exile) praise'd be instead! And for what, comrades, do we praise her?"

MUZHIK #4: "This man has a disease!"

MUZHIK #5: "God in Heaven! Help me—quickly—with this pillow, we'll smother him!"

MUZHIK #4: "No, no, no, you don't understand—they have found a cure!"

MUZHIK #5: "Halleluiah! A cure! I didn't understand—but now I do!"

MUZHIK #4: "Now you understand!"

MUZHIK #6: "Understand what?"

MUZHIK #5: "This man has a disease!"

MUZHIK #6: "Anathema!!"

MUZHIK #3: "But there is a cure!"

MUZHIK #6: "Glory be to God!"

MUZHIK #5: "Glory be! Now, if you could just help me with this pillow, I—"

MUZHIK #2: "We don't need the pillow—he's going to live!"

MUZHIK #1: "There is a *cure!*"

MOSIAGA: "There *is* a cure!"

RASKOLNIKOV: "Well . . . maybe I just don't even want your silly, old cure, anyway . . . did you ever think of that?!"

MUZHIK #6: "Egads, man!"

MOSIAGA: "But why? Why, Raskolnikov?! Why don't you want to live?"

MUZHIK #5: "If we could just find a good, fluffy pillow . . . what, what— one here just a moment ago . . ."

RASKOLNIKOV: "Tell me then—tell me, Mosiaga Nuninovich—would you want to live if your body was filled with poison!? Tainted! Tarnished with filthy, black, bilious heinousness!"

MOSIAGA: "Well . . . no, I suppose not . . . but—the cure . . ."

RASKOLNIKOV: "I don't mean the disease . . ."

MOSIAGA: "Then what?"

RASKOLNIKOV: "I am possessed by an unholy shadow!"

MOSIAGA: "Oh, yes, you did mention something about that . . ."

RASKOLNIKOV: "It's true! I know you'll think me mad—but it's all true! The sins I carry on my soul . . . the defiling debaucheries I have enacted in the consummate corrupting of my corporeity . . ."

MOSIAGA: "Lovely alliteration, though . . ."

RASKOLNIKOV: "Thank you."

MOSIAGA: "But—surely there must be something that can be done . . . and anyway, what could be so bad? Aside from your incessant squawking about it, you seem just fine to me . . ."

RASKOLNIKOV: "That's because *he* is sleeping—the spirit within me . . . he—well . . . I made suit to the lovely maid Nadia . . ."

MOSIAGA: "The chick on the balcony a couple of streets over?"

RASKOLNIKOV: "Yes, that's the one . . . and . . . well, it didn't go so well. So Vronsky—"

MOSIAGA: "That's the spirit? The name seems familiar . . ."

RASKOLNIKOV: "Well, no doubt he has possessed others before . . ."

MOSIAGA: "Ah, yes, that's probably it . . ."

RASKOLNIKOV: "So Vronsky poured tremendous amounts of vodka into me, and then threw me to the lions!"

MOSIAGA: "But this is Russia! There are no lions here . . . perhaps you meant he threw you to the bears?"

RASKOLNIKOV: "I was speaking metaphorically . . . in reality, he threw me to the whores!!"

MOSIAGA: "I see . . . but, I have to tell you, I can think of worse fates . . ."

RASKOLNIKOV: "Oh, but they were so . . . so. . .! And *thorough*! And then my . . . well—you know . . ."

MOSIAGA: "Your . . . 'little tsar'?"

RASKOLNIKOV: "Exactly! My little tsar retracted into me, and refused to be coaxed back out!"

MOSIAGA: "As if Ivan VI, locked away in the Schlusselberg Fortress . . ."

RASKOLNIKOV: "Well, I actually thought more of Peter III at Ropsha . . ."

MOSIAGA: "Yes, but the Ivan VI scenario is imbrued, as well, with the debilitation of sanity suffered from a life of imprisonment, so—"

RASKOLNIKOV: "Ah, yes, the debilitation of sanity—that's very true . . . I was looking at it from the point of view of a deposed tsar—whereas Ivan VI never actually ruled . . . but, yes, I have to agree that yours is the better analogy . . . butanyhoo . . ."

MOSIAGA: "So your monkey don't shine no more, hey?"

RASKOLNIKOV: "Oh, but such is merely the birth of my woes!"

MOSIAGA: "*Really?!* You're a very complex fellow . . ."

RASKOLNIKOV: "I have many levels . . ."

MOSIAGA: "Apparently . . . okay, so your schmecky wouldn't *yoo-hoo!* . . . then what?"

RASKOLNIKOV: "Vronsky dragged us to a priest—and forced the holy father to perform transubstantiation on my little tsar . . ."

MOSIAGA: "And he did this because . . .?"

RASKOLNIKOV: "So that—oh, God have mercy!—so that it would always rise again! Woe upon woe upon woe! My Penis is the body of Christ!!"

MOSIAGA: "Praise be to Your Penis!"

RASKOLNIKOV: "And also to yours."

MOSIAGA: "But that's really bloody awful!"

RASKOLNIKOV: "I know! I know! How could he have done such a thing?!"

MOSIAGA: "Yeah well, that, too—but I was actually referring to the joke in the writing itself . . . that's pretty bad . . ."

RASKOLNIKOV: "Yeah . . . but the author believes you've got to use up the easy ones, too . . ."

MOSIAGA: "Ah, yes . . . I guess I can see that . . . still—oh, well, nevermind. What were we saying?"

RASKOLNIKOV: "My Penis is the incarnation of God on Earth . . ."

MOSIAGA: "That's right! Would that make your testes like apostles?"

RASKOLNIKOV: "And I've now cured 40 sluts and 40 whores from the clap—merely by giving them *what's-what!*"

MOSIAGA: "Yikes!! You've got to be kidding me!"

RASKOLNIKOV: "If only I were . . . but I filled them all with the blood of Christ—literally!"

MOSIAGA: "You mean instead of . . .? Kinky!"

RASKOLNIKOV: "Wrought with the divine and carnal ecstasies of my accosting of them!"

MOSIAGA: "Accosting, hey? So with every five you'd have a 'Pentecost'!"

RASKOLNIKOV: "Oh no, now, you see—*that* was truly bad . . ."

MOSIAGA: "Okay, all right . . . that really was pretty bad . . . but you're still the guy pissing through God . . ."

RASKOLNIKOV: "What can I do, Mosiaga? The holy rite of transubstantiation cannot be undone!"

MOSIAGA: "And that guy with the pillow probably wouldn't be much help . . ."

RASKOLNIKOV: "I am lost!"

MOSIAGA: ". . . what if . . ."

RASKOLNIKOV: "What if what? Tell me if you have a solution!"

MOSIAGA: "Well, it's just that . . . what if you . . . you know—nailed It to a board?"

RASKOLNIKOV: "*Hmm . . . hmmm . . .* I think perhaps this has gone on far enough. Perhaps best to just stop now . . ."

MOSIAGA: "*HA!*—it's gone on too far already! You might as well see where it all ends up—you're already going to Hell . . ."

RASKOLNIKOV: "Indeed."

MOSIAGA: "Though, I suppose it's safe to say, your Penis will be saved . . ."

RASKOLNIKOV: "Oh! I hadn't thought of that—but I suppose you're right . . . my Penis should still go to Heaven . . . I wonder, will It grow little wings and a halo? Perhaps learn to play the harp?"

MOSIAGA: "Yeah, I don't know . . . maybe best to just move on to Scene 3 . . ."

RASKOLNIKOV: "Oh, indubitably, indubitably . . ."

[Both exit in opposite directions.]

Scene 3

[RASKOLNIKOV enters the wilderness (POTEMKIN in his head); bleak landscape of hellish red lighting and heinous black shadows . . . there is a bloody spot on the front of RASKOLNIKOV's pants, and he carries his penis nailed to a board.]

RASKOLNIKOV: "Heinousness unbounded! Holy crud! Holy goddamned pus, but that hurt!! And, yet, I sense the divinity of my genitals has been undone . . . and I sense . . . something—but what could it be? Is Vronsky, along with the essence of Christ, now gone from my being? I feel it to be true—I feel his death within me *(though wisps of his lingering spirit yet tickle a bit in some of my fancier places . . .).* But there is something amiss! Some new force has entered into play within . . ."

POTEMKIN: {This is me, then—so who are you now?}

RASKOLNIKOV: "Hidden voices surround! Who goes there?! Speak, whether thou be spirit, beast or man!"

POTEMKIN: {Near and far, near or far—never so near as seems so clear—never so far an to be where you are! What manner of me as I am? All you have named—but, mayhaps, the middlest by most . . .}

RASKOLNIKOV: "So I have traded up phallic godhood only to be possessed by the Beast himself?!? I want my penis back! Vronsky! Vronsky, can you hear me?! Rid my mind and soul of this beast, and I'll gladly be your Earthly slave!"

POTEMKIN: {That one now can help you not . . .} *[Belches with meaty profundity.]* {However, great nourishment have I found an his soulful substance. And, anyway, I am not '*the* Beast'. . . merely '*a* beast'—by name, Potemkin—ravager of souls!}

RASKOLNIKOV: "O nefarious spirit, I beg you—release me! Holy Virgin, blessed be!. . . save me in this, my hour of need! Forgive me my trespasses— for it was not my will to have made my penis the body of Christ, and, thus, the very fruit of your womb!"

POTEMKIN: {Ach! As lichen to me is she such—and unto my putrescence so shall I sweep, her bare an' bleeding essence so shall she weep! That one, too, can save you not! For you are held in sway by another *she*—a greater *she (if you ask it, me)* . . . the she **Kali**—mistress of sex and death! Mine infernal, belov'd Goddess!}

RASKOLNIKOV: "Well, this can't be good . . ."

POTEMKIN: {Always know where your holes are—else airy ere you spill!}

RASKOLNIKOV: "If only I had been stronger—able to control Vronsky's impulsive nature . . . perhaps heart and hand of the beauteous Nadia could have been won, and with the aid of her strength, so passionate and pure, we could have banished all such infectious spirits!"

POTEMKIN: {Innocence masqueraded fails to convince—hungers run rampant! *Amok!!* And amuster'd, forces to dally—diddly daring doo! I take her up onto mine horns, there to toss her all about—she is screaming!}

RASKOLNIKOV: "Nadia!?!"

POTEMKIN: {*Egads!*, but does she scream . . . 'til mine ears bleed—pulse pounding, heart thumping, blood surging, hungers exploding—succulent flesh, juicy marrow! But 'twas not for she to be—and so, too, 'twas not the one what were ere me . . . by dark-light of somniferously omnifarious moon—unripe fruition beckoned forth the Goddess and her glories! Whence Xalmoxis' servant basked in aftering void of potatoey-nectared undoing, 'twas simply enacted for **Kali**, in the moment of your undivining, to put me where vagarious Vronsky had been! —*Snatchity!*—*Snatchity!*—***BOOOM!!***— An' then they all—*a'come'a'tumblin' dowwwn!...*}

RASKOLNIKOV: "And so now, through you, your goddess claims me for her own?"

POTEMKIN: {Gilded illusion blinding in brilliance unfounded—caressing with wanting warmth of wicked wiles! She flees—I follow! Her sweat stinks life into my gluttony, and I leap down—catching her, ignoring flailing limbs as I fling her on high, there to toss her all about upon mine horns! And—}

RASKOLNIKOV: "Yes, yes, all up upon your horns—I get it! Infernal beast, ravager of souls—fine! Talk me to death already. Now, is Nadia all right? Or did you eat her?"

POTEMKIN: {She is not of concern. Besides—}

RASKOLNIKOV: "Besides what?"

POTEMKIN: {I am, as I have said, spirit as well as beast . . . Vronsky's spirit I could consume—but to, in actuality, consume another physical being . . .}

RASKOLNIKOV: "You would need an instrument to act through . . . namely—"

POTEMKIN: {Thou, aye . . . so if thou'rt picking her not from thy teeth, the wench, doubtless, yet lives undigested.}

RASKOLNIKOV: "Neat. So what does **Kali** want with me?"

POTEMKIN: {All the greater beings desire the warm, soft, deliciousness of humans—whe'r to devour or debauch . . . that thy penis was sanctified makes it all the more alluring. An the deed were done, **Kali** knew swiftly must her claim enacted be . . . Isis was hot on her heals—an' that haughty bitch doth harbor quite the little fetish for dismembered deified members! But all for naught, now that *we*—aye, wi' thee by me—are sworn in sex and death to terrible, tantalizing **Kali**!!}

[RASKOLNIKOV runs in circle, screaming, beating his head with the penis board, as POTEMKIN's maniacal laughter echoes all around; RASKOLNIKOV finally slumps to the ground unconscious.]

[Fade to black.]

Scene 4

[POTEMKIN enters (GROZNYI in his head); lush, green scenery from Scene 1, but with red lighting; when GROZNYI speaks, stage goes black, except single, brilliant white light over POTEMKIN/(GROZNYI).]

POTEMKIN: "Heave ho!—an the 'Raskol' be dead! *(Mama had a baby, an' off came the head!)* Mark me—mark me well!—for in mine whiling wiles I waited 'til the telling time, O Goddess bless'd be!—praise unto thy devoted Potemkin! *(He's worth more sorrow and that I'll spend on him!)* The epicurean essence of the dandy's duffer undone—turned to mine hungers own!—but sickly sweet dessert o'er the substance of corporeal consumption! Inspire us with the spleen of fiery dragons! The fop and the fool! *(Watching Jenny drool!)* Now shalt be I the primary—an' the *sole!* Hence!—wilt thou lift up Olympus?! On up onto mine horns!—flung far unto chaos an' dissolution! Ravager of all and of every! None e'er to supplant him! Ne'er an to recant him! Untouched by time, unhindered by barriers betwixt the myriad of realms!—by Infinity's decree of the will of **Kali**—"

GROZNYI: ^Hold on, now hold on there—don't just go counting chickens here . . .^

[Stage goes black.]

finis.

From Alexander Pushkin's 'Eugene Onegin' - II 39

. . . translated (and/or interpreted) by MFZ

"Revel as the years fly by
withal the fragility of life, my friends!
Beyond knowing of its worthlessness,
yet am I held within its sway . . .
to dreams and spectres I close my eyes—
though deep stirrings of hope, sometimes,
alight within my heart . . .
without some noticeable trace,
I would be saddened to leave this world . . .
and so I live, I write—not for praise,
but because I wish, perhaps,
to add to my sad fate some remembrance . . .
a last, lingering note—an if the truest friend—
e 'er to recollect the resonance of my song."

About the Author

A native of Wisconsin, Mishka Zakharin earned a Bachelor of Arts in English at the University of Wisconsin at Whitewater, where he was the recipient of the Jack Heide Award for Creative Writing. His writing influences are an eclectic mix of the greats of 19th Century Russian literature; Shakespeare, Marx (specifically Groucho), Jack Kerouac and Steve Martin. Zakharin's fiction and poetry have appeared in numerous anthologies and eBooks and he is currently working on his third novel, of which he says, "I really, really, really hope I finish this one…"

Previous Appearances

'The Siberian Saga' *(expurgated)*
No More Shall Be Said of This, Infinity Publishing © 2009

'In the Land of White Death'
Mishka's Florilegium, Infinity Publishing © 2006

'Chekhov's Pony'
Year of the Golden Monkey, Authorhouse Publishing © 2005

'Anna Karenina'
Of Gilded Hearts and Girded Loins, Booksurge Publishing © 2002

'Reading From Tolstoy'
Year of the Golden Monkey, Authorhouse Publishing © 2005
& *Mishka's Florilegium*, Infinity Publishing © 2006

'Ludmila of Tverskaya Street'
Banana You!, Authorhouse Publishing © 2003

'Big Julie's Radish Entourage'
That Was a Good Two Glopsworth, Infinity Publishing
© 2008 & *The Spleen of Fiery Dragons*, Infinity Publishing © 2009

'The 13ᵗʰ Apostle
The Masticator! (or: Chew On This For Awhile! . . .), Smashwords © 2010

'Le Morte de Vronsky'
Spectre of Life, Infinity Publishing © 2007; from Alexander
Pushkin's 'Eugene Onegin'–II 39, *Spectre of Life*, Infinity Publishing © 2007

Also Written by Mishka Zakharin

Big, Naughty Monkey
Of Gilded Hearts and Girded Loins
The Mad God
Mishka Shakespeare: The Complete Works
Mishka's Decameron
The Mishkan Book of the Dead
And Then She Put Her Clothes On and Left…
Mishka, Mishka
Mishka's Comedia *(2nd Edition)*
Bastard Imagery in Shakespeare
Big, Mad, Naughty Monkey God
Kromeshnik
Mishka's Florilegium
Sex and Death: Passion's Welts
The Spleen of Fiery Dragons

Chronicles of the Daemon Mishka:
Vol. I – Possessed By the Daemon Mishka
Vol. II – BANANA YOU!
Vol. III – Year of the Golden Monkey
Vol. IV – Spectre of Life
Vol. V – That Was a Good Two Glopsworth
Vol. VI – No More Shall Be Said of This…

Zakharin's eBooks on Smashwords:
Zakharinish Zeitgeist
The Vodka Diaries
The Masticator! *(or: Chew On This For Awhile!...)*
Kriego Silencieux…!
Enigmatatas and Eclecticicities
The Brighter Side of Angst

The Official Mishka Zakharin Website: www.mishkazakharin.com

www.ingramcontent.com/pod-product-compliance
Lightning Source LLC
Chambersburg PA
CBHW070845120626
46556CB00002B/885